"Fickett's careful historical context ex[Jesus' parables were so disturbing to his listeners, but his next step makes them equally disturbing today by recasting those stories in contemporary language and situations. Readers may catch themselves reacting: 'Surely Jesus didn't mean that!'" He did, though.

DORIS BETTS,
author of *The Sharp Teeth of Love*

"Harold Fickett, a gifted writer, has produced a wonderfully readable and provocative book, which brings to life many of Jesus' parables. As always, Harold makes us think, disturbs us, but in the end, moves us."

CHARLES W. COLSON,
chairman of Prison Fellowship Ministries

"Harold Fickett's thoughtful, probing dialog with Jesus' parables helps me understand just how disturbing these teachings were—and are. *Conversations with Jesus* will reward careful reading and re-reading."

TIM STAFFORD,
senior writer for *Christianity Today* magazine, and author of
Knowing the Face of God and *The Stamp of Glory*

"*Conversations with Jesus* is a primer in human response to divine initiatives. With uncanny perception and insight, its author penetrates the meaning of the parables of Jesus. Thoroughly conversant with the intricate varieties of human behavior, Fickett, in his modern retelling of these Jesus-stories, not only demonstrates his gifts as a powerful writer of fiction, he bring us slap-up against some of our own wrong-headed motivations and actions. Salutary and transformative reading,"

LUCI SHAW,
poet and author of *Writing the River* and *Water to My Soul*

HAROLD FICKETT

CONVERSATIONS WITH JESUS

Unexpected Answers to Contemporary Questions

PIÑON PRESS

P.O. Box 35007, Colorado Springs, Colorado 80935

OUR GUARANTEE TO YOU

We believe so strongly in the message of our books that we are making this quality guarantee to you. If for any reason you are disappointed with the content of this book, return the title page to us with your name and address and we will refund to you the list price of the book. To help us serve you better, please briefly describe why you were disappointed. Mail your refund request to: Piñon Press, P.O. Box 35002, Colorado Springs, CO 80935.

ISBN 1-57683-034-9

Cover design by David Uttley Design
Illustration by Jon Conrad
Creative Team: Brad Lewis, Eric Stanford, Terry Behimer, Tim Howard, Steve Eames, Melissa Munro

Harold Fickett's personal stories are true to life. All other illustrations are either wholly invented or composites of real situations, and any resemblance to people living or dead is coincidental.

ONE OF US, by Eric Bazilian
© 1995, 1996 Human Boy Music (ASCAP)
All Rights Administered by WB Music Corp.
All Rights Reserved. Used by Permission.
WARNER BROS. PUBLICATIONS U.S. INC., Miami, FL. 33014

Fickett, Harold.
        Conversations with Jesus : unexpected answers to contemporary
    questions / Harold Fickett.
            p.   cm.
        ISBN 1-57683-034-9
        1. Christian life.   I. Title.
    BV4501.2.F475   1999
    248.4—dc21   99-38112
                                                                          CIP

Unless otherwise identified, all Scripture quotations in this publication are taken from the *New Revised Standard Version* (NRSV), copyright © 1989 by the Division of Christian Education of the National Council of the Churches of Christ in the USA, used by permission, all rights reserved. Other versions used include: *The Message: New Testament with Psalms and Proverbs* (MSG) by Eugene H. Peterson, copyright © 1993, 1994, 1995, used by permission of NavPress Publishing Group; the *New King James Version* (NKJV), copyright © 1979, 1980, 1982, 1990, Thomas Nelson Inc., Publishers; the *King James Version* (KJV); the *New Jerusalem Bible* (NJB) copyright © 1985 by Darton, Longman & Todd, Ltd., and Doubleday & Company, Inc.

Printed in the United States of America

1 2 3 4 5 6 7 8 9 10 11 12 13 14 15 / 05 04 03 02 01 00 99

For the conversations with Jesus
of the two Harolds before me.

CONTENTS

SECTION I
LOVING

CHAPTER ONE

OPENING

"I FEEL SO DEAD INSIDE."

I remember, and will always remember, groaning out this truth in a Houston alcoholic rehabilitation hospital before I knew what I had said, even as the fullness of this realization draped black bunting over the closed windows and doors of my soul. I was alive but dead. I had known about the fear, the depression, and the anger—and the addictions to alcohol and prescription drugs that were their medium—but only in speaking these very words did I learn the full truth.

I had only one question: "Where is God?"

Like many people, I waited to ask this question until absolutely nothing made sense anymore. Perhaps that's the moment in each of our lives when the question gets asked with all the immediacy and heartfelt longing it deserves.

Where is God? Alone at 4 A.M. or beside a family member's deathbed, most of us ask this question. Whether we are young people learning for the first time how cruel the world can be, or adults grieving over personal failure or friends' betrayal, *Where is God?* rides the whirlwind.

I was a longtime Christian, even a "professional Christian" — someone who wrote and taught about the faith — and yet, if there was any power in the faith I had embraced, I had rendered it null and void ten years ago. Now I had to begin all over again. My despair brought me back to the perennial questions, which are always the questions of youth. Where is God? Can I know him? In what way? If I can know God, will I choose to? Will I have to change? In my case, of course, I could only hope I would change. So I went on to ask, How can I change or be changed in order to live again?

Then I wondered, What kind of person might I become? Who will I be?

As I renewed my search for answers to these questions, I clung at first to the faith my parents, thank heavens, bred into my bones. By that light, I recognized I had to stop drinking and start praying like I meant it, and I began walking a long road back to health and sanity.

Several years later when I finally found myself, so to speak, sane, clothed, and in my right mind, I wanted a much deeper experience of personal and spiritual renewal. I wanted not only to be "well-adjusted" in a psychotherapeutic sense, but to live as fully and effectively as I had hoped as a teenager: to be so caught up into seeking God that I would experience an utterly transforming belief. It seemed that for this to come about I had to reexamine the most basic questions. Did I really know what the Christian faith was about? In my life as a "professional Christian" I couldn't have known very deeply, not in the way that transformed the lives of people like St. Augustine and St. Francis; gentle poets like George Herbert; the missionary to China Hudson Taylor; and near-contemporaries like Thomas Merton, C. S. Lewis, and Mother Teresa. Whatever such figures believed, it made a big difference in their lives and in their world, the kind of difference that people from every tradition can respect. Even skeptics applaud the motivations and caring work that a few of Jesus' followers have sustained.

Which brought me back to thinking about Jesus, because

my faith, the Christian faith, is about him. When it's not about him, as I'd proven to myself, it's about nothing—or maybe throwing oneself into nothingness. If I wanted to experience renewal, I had to draw closer to Jesus. I knew that much.

When I thought of undertaking the same quest in the past, first as a teenager and then in the midst of my unraveling, I found myself facing common problems that shunted me into blind alleys. If Christianity is to be believed, we have prayer and the Scriptures, yes, as a direct means of access to Jesus, but we live in a culture permeated by such skepticism that it's difficult to trust our faithful perceptions. We live with questions about Jesus that are new or at least seem new. How might I pose these questions in a way that does justice to the times that have formed me? And how would I seek for answers in prayer, in the Scriptures, and in commentary about Jesus in a way that might come up with real answers, transforming answers? I wanted not merely to find the truth of the matter, but to live the truth. No more living death for me, thank you, but life that is truly life.

After all, I had been given a second chance to live. I could not blow it this time because I knew now, as I did not know when I was young, how much time takes away from us: possibilities truly can become impossible.

As I began my own search for renewal, I realized that my inquiry was one small manifestation of a global phenomenon. The spiritual longings of our world make news, both good and bad, from the liberation of Eastern Europe, which was spurred to a great degree by Christian priests and ministers, to death cults in Japan.[1] The word *spirituality* is currently in favor. In dominant Western cultural media, skepticism prevails regarding "religion," and speaking of any one religion—Judaism, Buddhism, Christianity, or Islam—strikes the ear as too particular, too exclusive. But talking of one's "spirituality" receives an open hearing. A great spiritual renewal is under way.

The new spirituality shuns the old language. Key words from the old religions are suspect: words like "redemption," "righteousness," even "holiness." Just toss 'em. People can no longer relate. These words communicate fear and judgment, not comfort and acceptance. For many, if not most, the old language obscures the very truths cherished by people who still understand this vocabulary.

Likewise, my old ways of talking about God, everything from choruses learned as a child in Sunday school to fading echoes of a hundred thousand sermons, kept returning me to the truth as I had known it, even though I had proved—to my own satisfaction and that of those around me—that the truth as I had known it made precious little difference in real life.

Still, I began to hope that if I could hit upon a satisfying method of conducting my search, it would have some value for others as well. We are all up against similar problems, especially this problem of finding new ways of talking about spiritual matters.

For example, what comes to mind when one says "Jesus"? In our culture, quite a mix of associations, from polite regard for the good moral teacher to the figurehead of one's cultural enemies. Some think of crazy redneck preachers on the radio (for whom I have a particular fondness, by the way) or smarmy televangelists. Others have more serious concerns because of centuries of anti-Semitism and the Church's abuse of great thinkers like Galileo. Powerful negative associations work against any new consideration of Jesus, especially the idioms and images used by cultural opponents. Jesus actually tends to be obscured by all the worn-out, dull commentary about him, his true image written over so much that he has been penciled into a big, dark lead box.

But I had to think about Jesus—both my reborn faith and its dark legacy demanded it. And I think our culture needs to think about Jesus too, if only to reconcile itself with dimensions of Jesus' teaching that remain hugely, if often subtly, influential. Although people within Western society share less and less in terms of a common intellectual tradition, speaking of a wayward child as a "prodigal son" summons a host of instant associations. Newspaper headlines and stories still use the short-hand of the "Good Samaritan." Even the short sayings of Jesus—blessed are the poor, those who mourn, the pure in heart, the peacemakers—continue to direct our thinking. Our cultural memories of what Jesus actually said remain positive.

What I really wished I could do, I came to see, would be to trail after Jesus, as his followers and the crowds did, and ask him questions. I wanted to ask him today's questions, with all their built-in skepticism and despairing weight.

The impossibility of this seemed all the more frustrating because Jesus' original audience took full advantage of their opportunity to ask the questions in their hearts. In fact, the more I read the original accounts of Jesus (the Gospels of Matthew, Mark, Luke, and John) the more I saw that Jesus' teachings, especially the short fictions, the parables, came in reply to questions. One of the disciples or someone in the crowd asked a question, and Jesus told a story in response. After-ward, he would sometimes expand on the meaning of the story with short wisdom sayings. In a few rare instances, he explained the story's meaning (or one of its meanings) directly to the dis-ciples, at least if we are to believe the Gospel accounts.[2]

As I began to investigate and think about the parables and short sayings of Jesus, I realized—with a start—that Jesus composed them. At some point, either before his public ministry in Joseph's house or in retreat to pray or on his teaching journeys, Jesus made the parables up. These are *his* stories. My own writing and reading of fiction has taught me—sometimes to my embarrassment—that one's stories allow the reader access into the writer's deepest imagination. The reader can't always tell what's autobiographical and what's not—I don't mean that. What I mean is that the reader can tell what the writer thinks about the nature of the world: his or her approach to reality.

The parables and short sayings are Jesus' comments on what's real and what's not in life. They are his means of inter-preting the world, of explaining the world and God's action in it to his questioners. They also show how God's action in the world is being realized through Jesus' own mission. Of course I realize, as some skeptics may be eager to interject, that the original books about Jesus, the Gospels, are not court reporter transcriptions of his teachings and actions. The evangelists have their purposes, which they exhibit through their selection of materials, the arrangement of those materials, and the Gospel writers' individual variations of Jesus' teachings. In addition, scholars have debated how much of the material in the Gospels comes from Jesus himself and how much from the original writers and their subsequent editors.

Nearly everyone agrees, however, that the stories and sayings that continue to influence our collective mind come from Jesus himself. So I determined that the parables and short sayings are definitely the place to begin any fresh investigation of Jesus' teaching — the most widely appealing place to begin. No one need be put off. We all have our own investments in these passages.

So I kept wondering whether there might be a way to insert myself and my own concerns and the questions of our time into the Gospel picture of people asking Jesus questions and receiving his parables and wisdom sayings in reply.

But if I did that, the parables would have to be different ones, wouldn't they? The parables depend so much for their meanings, as I was learning, on the audience's frame of reference. Much, if not everything, lies in their details.

That question essentially generated this work, because I saw that composing new parables after Jesus' own — making up new parables based on close attention to the originals and in the hope of catching something of the original parables' inspiration — would draw me into Jesus' reasoning imagination; in many respects, that's a way of getting even closer to someone than by talking in the flesh.

By asking my questions, searching the Gospels for what might have been Jesus' answers, and composing parables that reflect, in our time and circumstances, how Jesus might have replied, I seemed to hit upon a means of engaging Jesus anew.

This would be my own way of talking to him, of carrying on a conversation at a profound level. I would try responding to his message as a jazz saxophonist might respond with his own improvisations to the compositions of his master. Might I come to feel as if I were carrying on a duet, my stories as a harmonizing line to Jesus'—or at least a descant?

As I began to hear Jesus' answers to my questions in the composition of new parables, I began finding the themes of that transforming belief for which I longed. I became convinced that I understood Jesus as I never had before—to the point of having an immediate sense of the man himself. I don't mean to imply any mystical encounters because I had none, but in trying to give a sense of the power I felt in this, I might compare it to having a private conference with a beloved teacher. Where once I was in the back benches, now I was standing right next to him, and he was replying directly to me. Or, to put it another way, when asked in previous years why I was a Christian, I usually said something about Christianity making more sense of life than other ways of thinking. I'm inclined now simply to answer, "him." That's how intimate I felt these conversations became.

I want to say this, too, as both encouragement and warning to the reader: Believe or disbelieve, Jesus met in anything like his furious authenticity must awaken us to our commitments, our allegiances, to all the meanings our own stories possess. As we come to understand these things about ourselves, we also see the necessity of answering his own preeminent question: "Who do you say that I am?" To answer this question with all of our hearts cannot help but dispose those hearts toward something greater than happiness or self-fulfillment or even peace and security; such a decision becomes, for better or worse, destiny.

What follows then are conversations with Jesus through today's questions, then stories that are contemporary transformations of Jesus' originals, and finally meditations on how the two stories connect with each other and our world.

There's no flimflam presumption here that Jesus dictated the replies or even took responsibility for improving my storytelling ability. Plunging into the creativity with which Jesus constructed his parables has been humbling—one among the many aspects of these conversations that has caused me to rethink everything.

CHAPTER TWO

IS THERE A
LOVING GOD?

IF WE ARE GOING TO BRING OUR DEEPEST SELVES TO A CON-
versation with Jesus, there's no escaping a first, almost pre-
emptive, overwhelming doubt: Does God exist? And, more
particularly, is God personal? Is there a loving God?

Our culture's legacy of disbelief has formed each of us. We
may like thinking of ourselves as "spiritual" people, but even
the Amish must grow up these days with an interior voice
that keeps whispering, *Nobody believes that anymore.*

I remember being in graduate school, where my profes-
sors and peers sometimes regarded (and pitied) me as the
poster child Christian. One afternoon, at a party in a student
couple's apartment, the host was playing with his baby daughter. The little girl was lying on her back. The young father put
his face down to hers until their noses touched and then he
quickly raised his head, popped his eyes, and said, "Boo!" to
his child's screaming delight.

The professor with whom we were all working stood by
me, and he remarked on the young father's game, "There,
Harold, that's God."

He meant that God is merely a projection of each person's need to feel cared for. Two centuries ago the philosopher Feurbach said essentially the same thing. In the nineteenth century Nietzsche proclaimed God dead, and in the twentieth even theologians began thinking they should take their cues from unbelief.

Despite these trends in philosophy, belief in God, if the American polls are to be believed, remains high. (This is less true of Europe, but true to an even greater degree in the Third World.) But can anyone doubt that our confidence in God, and especially the extent to which the individual can know God, has been shaken? Even the notion of a common reality—the idea of truth itself—has suffered. Many believe there is no objective truth, no truth that transcends time and culture. Most intellectuals are preoccupied with the cultural and historical contexts for ideas, which, many claim, belong so completely to these contexts that they have no validity beyond them. What's true in Western European culture of the twenty-first century would be false to Margaret Mead's famous Trobiand Islanders. As Kurt Vonnegut might add, "So it goes," with the despairing implication that there's no way to tell how it *should* go.

The average person seems influenced by these trends to the degree that he or she prefers to keep ideas about God private and to assume that one's private ideas don't necessarily apply to others. God can exist for me, if not for you, and we'd really better not talk about it.

In addition to the skeptical philosophers, for the last fifty years scientists have been preaching that the universe, as far as we can know, came about by chance. Currently, the notion of "chaos studies" has everyone in thrall; we seem delighted at dispensing with order itself—or embracing the notion that disintegration can have creative effects. The contemporary mind echoes with the late Carl Sagan's pronouncement, "The Cosmos is all that is or ever was or ever will be." [1] Sagan's cosmos is too big for God and any notion of design; it exists on its own terms, which are purposeless.

I'm not so much interested in the intellectual history of

all this as I am in the common prejudices that we bring to hearing the words of Jesus. What it's like to be a contemporary]person schooled in skepticism.

Or one who finds himself or herself in something more akin to an intellectual double whammy—a doubt so pervasive that God, when he rises to the level of consciousness at all, becomes an engaging whimsy.

> What if God were one of us?
> Just a slob like one of us?
> Just a stranger on a bus try'n to make his way home.[2]

These popular lyrics reflect a state of mind in which belief and unbelief might be difficult to distinguish. Young people and many others in our culture seem to have given up on old-fashioned skepticism in exchange for a general permission to believe anything and everything, without any means of distinguishing truth from falsehood. Beliefs are goods to be consumed and discarded according to individual appetites. Notions that are absolutely opposed to one another—like the existence of God and his nonexistence—find an equal welcome within the same person. What might Jesus say to someone who saw his attitude to God's existence as one means among many of having fun?

Whether we bring toward the ultimate a disdainful philosophic skepticism, a scientific naturalism that makes God gratuitous, a consumerist playfulness, or simply a shyness about asking the big questions as a result of these influences, we have many doubts about the existence of a loving God. Even as someone with a long history of belief, that's what I brought to my own personal quest and still bring by virtue of day-to-day misgivings. Doubt is in the air I breathe.

The famous historian Paul Johnson says that everyone asks these two questions: Does God love us and does God act like it?

So I started wondering whether anyone had asked Jesus if there truly is a loving God and whether God acts accordingly. I wondered how Jesus answered these two questions—or might have.

THE CORVAIR AT MIDNIGHT

A MAN AND HIS FAMILY IN THEIR ANCIENT, MUFFLER-DRAGGING Corvair stopped at the entrance to a new gated community. The guard on duty asked them their business.

"My friend lives here," the man said. He handed the guard a letter.

The letter bore the right return address. It was written in someone's own hand and its first lines appeared friendly enough. The guard shone his flashlight into the Corvair's interior, where an obviously pregnant woman sat beside the driver, with two small boys, a spaghetti of arms and legs, asleep in the back.

"Your children should be wearing their seat belts," the guard said.

"You want me to wake them?" the woman asked.

"We're here for a visit," the driver said. "Mr. Danielson is expecting us. We had car trouble. That's why we're so late."

The guard could believe that. "OK. You take a right at the third street. Then an immediate left."

The Corvair pulled into the circular drive of the colonnaded home. The driver went up and rang the doorbell. He waited. He rang the doorbell again.

The door didn't open, but someone began talking to him. "Who is it? Who's there?"

The driver saw the beige intercom box at his right. He pushed the talk button. "It's Charlie. Charlie Laughlin."

"Charlie? Charlie, what are you doing here?"

"We thought we'd come for a visit." He coughed. "Your letter said anytime."

"Yeah, anytime, but Charlie, it's the middle of the night."

"Well, I'm sorry we're so late, but like you said, it's the middle of the night, so can we come in?"

"We?"

"The family. Gina and the kids are in the car. Gina may just drop the new one in the driveway at any moment if we don't. Can we come in?"

The intercom went silent for a moment. "Charlie," said the owner at last, "why don't you go to a motel or something? There's one just a block from the gate. They always have rooms. Come back in the morning and visit. We'll have a nice, long talk. Just now — it's the middle of the night, Charlie. I'll see you in the morning."

"Henry," the driver said. "Henry, did you understand what I said? Gina's pregnant and not feeling too well."

"In the morning, Charlie! Good night!"

Charlie stood at the door for a moment. If he could just wake Henry up enough so that he could see the situation in person. . . . He rang the doorbell. He knocked.

Finally, he went around to the back to see if he could knock on his friend's bedroom window. As he moved along the side of the house, floodlights snapped on, spot-lighting the area around him as if he were standing in a guard tower's searchlight. He couldn't see anything for a moment, but he heard a whooping siren that rose and fell. Then, as quickly as the alarm began, it stopped. The lights dropped.

Charlie began walking back toward the front of the house. His friend Henry met him as he was still picking his way along the pebbled side path.

"Charlie, what on earth are you doing?"

"Henry, I just thought if you saw me . . . Look Henry, it's me, Charlie."

Henry stroked his sleepy face with his hand, rubbed his eyes.

"We don't have anywhere else to go," Charlie said. "We're broke. I'm broke. I'm not sure there's enough gas in the Corvair to drive it away."

"Man, I know we're friends, but you are such a screw-up." A glare came into Henry's eye that pierced the darkness. "If you want to know, Denise and I made it official. We got married last month. She and the girls are living here now. In fact, we're taking the new family for an outing tomorrow. Disneyland. The whole bit. And that's no easy thing because the girls still resent our relationship. So you see I *can't* put you up tonight. I just can't, Charlie!"

Charlie shrugged as if to say, Well, what else am I going to do?

"Look, I'll give you gas money." Henry rolled his head back on his neck and looked to the stars for confirmation of what he had just said. "Then you go and you don't come back. Understand?"

"But we're friends," Charlie said. "We've been friends for twenty years!"

Henry turned and walked stiffly away, his T-shirt still hitched up high to one side of a boxer-shorted hip.

When Charlie reached the driveway, he saw the community patrolman's car, its lights on, throwing its high beams up against Henry's door. The security guard was bending over, talking to Gina. Several of Henry's neighbors on both sides of the street were standing on their porches. One and then another of the men started walking over to Henry's yard. Their wives shooed their kids back inside, while remaining on their porch steps, watching.

The security guard came up to Henry and Charlie. "Is this man a friend of yours, sir?" he asked.

"We've been friends for twenty years," Charlie said quickly. "There's no trouble here, officer."

Charlie, desperate, took the letter out from his back pocket. "See, I have a letter." Charlie cast his voice to the neighbors standing at the foot of the drive. "This is all a misunderstanding. I have a letter inviting us to visit."

"Are these people your guests, sir?" the guard asked.

Denise was suddenly at Henry's elbow. "What's going on?" she asked. "Who are these people?"

Charlie put his hand out. "Henry and I are friends from

college and the Guard. Glad to meet you. You're Denise, right? Actually we go back to high school. Gina's eight months along—I'm afraid she's not feeling too well."

"If these are your friends, Henry, we'd better get them inside. What are we doing out here?" Denise asked.

Finally, Henry said, "I'm sorry the alarm sounded, officer. I didn't expect my friends so late. It was just a false alarm. Then Charlie came around the side of the house to find me." Henry threw up his hands. "It got complicated."

"There's no trouble then?" the guard asked.

"Just you responding when you didn't have to," Henry said.

"That's okay," the guard said. "But you know there's a charge for alarm calls."

"I know. That's fine. Sorry about all this. Really sorry, believe me."

The Oxygen of the Spiritual World

FOR ALL OF US, LIFE IS KNOCKING ON DOORS. DOORS TO hearts, to jobs, to the darkness in which our anxieties, lost hopes, and destructive impulses hide. We are always on one threshold or another, with needs embarrassingly apparent.

My story shows us a man defined by blatant need— arriving in the middle of the night, his pregnant wife at some risk, his children exhausted.

How often in our own hearts are we defined in the same way? Perhaps at the deepest level we always are, for the illusion of the autonomous self-made man or woman ultimately gives way. We may live in such anxiety that we only stand at most doors, afraid to knock, and yet whichever way we turn, another door appears, confronting us with a choice that may be real or illusory. We live our lives wondering whether doors will open.

We know how many doors stay closed.

And yet, we feel that Denise's response is the right one: "If these are your friends, Henry, we'd better get them inside. What are we doing out here?"

One of the simplest — or shortest — of Jesus' stories exploits the response we have to Denise's question, opening up Jesus' understanding of God. Once, after Jesus had returned to his disciples after a time of private prayer, they asked him to teach them how to pray. In teaching them to pray, Jesus told them a story:

> "Suppose one of you has a friend, and you go to him at midnight and say to him, 'Friend, lend me three loaves of bread; for a friend of mine has arrived, and I have nothing to set before him.' And he answers from within, 'Do not bother me; the door has already been locked, and my children are with me in bed; I cannot get up and give you anything.' I tell you, even though he will not get up and give him anything because he is his friend, at least because of his persistence he will get up and give him whatever he needs. So I say to you, Ask, and it will be given you; search, and you will find; knock, and the door will be opened for you."[3]

This story counts heavily on the rich traditions of hospitality common to Judaism and the Middle East. These traditions of hospitality demanded that the sleeping householder respond immediately. The householder would have violated such an important taboo to the mind of Jesus' audience that they would have been shocked and horrified at his excuses. Jesus' audience might have laughed, if uncomfortably, at this story, taking it as a farce.

The deepest meanings of the story turn on one word, rendered in this version and many others as *persistence*. The word, *anaideia*, here translated "persistence," may instead mean "shamelessness," or perhaps simply the "avoidance of shame." It may even apply to the sleeping householder rather than the knocking friend. (The English translation I've used applies the term to the one who knocks; the original Greek text can be read either way.)

If "avoidance of shame" applies to the knocking friend, then the parable becomes a story about the friend's persistence or shamelessness in asking for what he knows the sleeping householder should provide. (And certainly our hero, Charlie, does his best along this line.) For the tenacious friend to call out more than once, for him to persist, will let the neighbors know of the householder's resistance and cause a scandal.

The story can then be used, as the early church used it (and as most of us today do as well), as an illustration of the need to persist in prayer. And certainly, as part of Jesus' teaching on prayer, that's an appropriate application.

But on the other hand, if we translate "persistence" as "to avoid shame" and apply it to the householder, then the parable becomes a different story altogether, one that stands as an ironic comparison between the sleeping householder and Jesus' vigilant Father.

The sleeping householder may act only to avoid shame in the eyes of his neighbors, but he will act—we can count on human expediency. Is that all we can count on? No. If the traditions of hospitality and communal pressure can motivate a facsimile of charitable behavior on the part of the scandalously unfriendly householder, how much more will the Father, who truly loves us, respond to our persistent requests. We are to expect this, Jesus says, to rely on it.

Like the shorter sayings Luke situates closely to it—"What father among you, if his son asked for a fish, would hand him a snake? Or if he asked for an egg, would hand him a scorpion?"—the parable evokes the immediate reply in Jesus' audience, "No one!" And it allows for the conclusion that Jesus draws: "If you then, who are evil, know how to give good gifts to your children, how much more will the heavenly Father give the Holy Spirit to those who ask him!"[4]

Jesus argues from the "little to the great," as other rabbis did. He takes the smallest possible example of charity or love, and then he uses this small thing to establish by analogy the great thing—the love of God. He reminds his audience that even the worst of their neighbors can be counted on for help, to act lovingly, if only for the sake of their reputations. If we can depend on mere human beings to act charitably in this way, as evil as we are, then we can absolutely count on the great thing, the goodness of God. His comparison uses the things of this world to give us information about what lies beyond this world.

Which set me thinking further about my own expectations and those of our world. What does our crowd of skeptics, scientific agnostics, and new age religious speculators expect? How do we react to having had this moment of conscience provoked (our response to Denise's question) and Jesus' sayings about his Father? It's strange, isn't it, that we know Denise asks the right question. If we know that much, why wouldn't God? Why wouldn't we count on God to know? Jesus says we can.

My own heart longs for God to behave in just the fashion Jesus indicates. But then I still have to reflect on my own expectations. Do I *expect* God to answer the contemporary doorbell?

Jesus encourages us to pray to a loving God—a generous Father—from whom we can expect a gracious reply. Do I expect such a reply from a loving Father?

Even this metaphor of the "Father" stops many today. The old language of piety and its "gracious heavenly Father" has come to seem oxymoronic—a contradiction in terms. We think of the world's unmerited suffering, starvation, disease, and the violence of nature and its catastrophes, and we wonder how a loving God, a gracious Father, can allow such devastation and pain. More commonly and personally, to us and to people of every age no doubt, the word "father" likely carries with it some measure of disappointment and perhaps betrayal. Few have been loved in the way they long to be, although there are happy exceptions. Most of us feel needs that our fathers have not and cannot meet—whether personal, financial, or in relation to our mothers, sisters, and brothers. Have we been abandoned or put off emotionally? Have our choices been condemned— something that can hurt even when we're not too sure of those choices ourselves?

But we must always come back to the fact that Jesus uses the metaphor of a gracious Father here, there, and everywhere, to the point of teaching us to pray to a Daddy ("Abba") in the Lord's prayer. We can throw this out as so much cultural baggage or we can try to appropriate the image in ways that give us access to its depths.

For many, this means reexamining fatherhood itself in terms of our own personal histories.

I readily admit to having had a father problem. For years I felt as if I never received the love that I wanted from my father and felt entitled to.

When I became a father the first time, I presumed my wife and I would have a girl. The moment my son was born, my immediate reaction was, "Oh no!" He and I are going to have to go through those terrible straits that I have yet to negotiate with my own dad. How am I going to be a proper father to him when I have yet to be a proper son?

My son was delivered after an excruciatingly painful twenty-four-hour labor. The medical team was about to perform an emergency C-section. The umbilical cord had actually wrapped around the baby's neck, and he was suffocating.

Just before the surgeon arrived, the attending physician tried one last crude measure. He ordered the nurse to get up on a step stool and push down "as hard as you can!" on my poor wife's abdomen.

"Now!" he commanded.

The nurse whomped down.

My son's shoulder finally cleared and he was delivered. His entire body was kidney-colored, the color of de-oxygenated blood. He looked like one massive boiled contusion. And his head, because of the narrow passage, was shaped like nothing so much as a summer squash.

I remember standing to the side of my wife's bed as the doctors worked over my newborn off to the left. My one thought was, He could die. This seemed so strange. My wife and he had come all this way. And now he was going to die?

I heard a spluttering choke and then a soft cry. Why didn't he wail?

The doctor brought him around the bed past me to a warming bath and invited me to look on. The nurse rocked him back and forth in the water—almost in the way I had rocked caught trout back and forth in the past to revive them—and soon a pink spot appeared right at the place of his heart. The pink skin tone radiated out from there, down along his legs, out to his hands, and finally it colored his cheeks. He started to cry beautifully.

Oh my boy, I thought, my son, my son. Welcome, welcome. I'm so glad you are here.

As oxygen spread through my son's body, the oxygen of the spiritual world—love—filled mine. Then I knew that I had been absolutely and completely wrong about my dad. I knew that behind all my adolescent resentment stood a father who loved me in exactly the way I loved this newborn. And I knew my son loved me, shockingly so. I knew that I had a huge treasure of grace in this inescapable love my son had for me and I for him and that I would have to be truly pathetic to mess this up.

And I knew that if he asked me for a piece of bread, I would buy him meals to last him all his life. If he asked me for a fish, I would buy him a trawler. And if he asked for an egg, I would hide Easter eggs for as long as he wanted to hunt them, and every brightly colored egg would stand for a trait of character or personal gift that I would help my son nurture and grow into.

This is what Jesus means when he tells us that we have a loving Father. He means that God feels for me—to an infinitely greater degree—what I felt for my son at his birth; Jesus calls us to ground all our expectations about life in this supreme reality. What we find in every loving relationship, between spouses, within families and friendships, speaks of God's overwhelming love for us. At the deep heart's core of the universe beats a heart that is love. Is there a loving God? According to Jesus, God not only acts like it but acts *in no other way*. God can't. It would betray God's character as a loving Father—the one thing God is incapable of doing. God's heart is bigger than the universe—even bigger than Mr. Sagan's cosmos because God's loving presence extends to its farthest boundary and well beyond.

It's hard to believe. Knowing what I do about how much I love my son Hal and his little brother Will and sister Eve, it's hard to fathom that much love. Nothing else that Jesus teaches makes any sense, though, if this is not true.

CHAPTER THREE

WHAT ABOUT
TRAGEDY?

ANY UNDERSTANDING OF LIFE, RELIGIOUS OR OTHERWISE, doesn't add up to much—and can result in huge losses—if it's not first of all realistic. After a moment of insight like I experienced at my son's birth or hearing Jesus' sayings about God's character as a loving Father—that God loves us and that God acts like it—we may feel transported for a time by a sense of reconciliation, only to find irritations and troubling memories stealing back to capture our attention once more.

Wait a minute. If we are to believe God loves us and expect him to give us good gifts, why are prayers for the simplest things in life, and often the most needful, left unanswered? Who cares, particularly, about being given a full dose of spiritual ecstasy when he's starving to death? What can such assurances mean to those who have been unjustly imprisoned—either by bars or ill health or disabilities? How can there truly be a loving God when life is so clearly tragic?

I find myself almost encamped in this objection when I meet up with spiritual people who are hysterics of one variety or another: those who have conferred a religious status on their wishful thinking and exist so blatantly in denial that I can hardly restrain myself from slapping them.

I'm referring to the fundamentalist who speaks of knowing God's will from moment to moment while being so depressed he can hardly get up in the morning; or the Catholic who believes invoking the aid of just the right saint will magically unlock the treasure trove of heavenly mercy for an ailing child; and the New Ager who confronts the breakup of his family with knowing smiles, implying a secret knowledge that makes this circumstance of no account. To all these and others like them: cut it out! I want nothing to do with any faith that asks me to choose between a full and honest humanity and an optimism constituted by willful blindness. Much better agnosticism than any false illusions.

I remember driving with my grandfather in his boxy Olds 88 after visiting my grandmother in the hospital. We were on a four-lane road with a wide dirt median. He hadn't spoken since we left the hospital, and I (then nine years old) waited for him to keep his adult thoughts to himself or unfold them as he liked. He did neither. He pulled abruptly into the dirt median, stopped the car with a forward-rocking plunge, and then buried his face in his hands as he began to sob and cry. I remember how *loud* his grief sounded. "Oh, your grandma is so sick, Tiger," he said to me. "Your grandmother is so sick."

My grandfather, after an early career as a chemist, had turned to preaching. He was certainly one of the most faithful and soulful believers I have ever known. Besides the prayers I heard directly, I'm sure he prayed "without ceasing" for my grandmother's recovery. He was devoted to her, being wise enough to understand that her love had sustained and lifted him toward whatever he had accomplished in life and, in sum, made him.

My grandmother died not long afterward.

A good gift?

Death is not the worst outcome, death is part of life, blah, blah, blah.

Save it. The crushing grief that hits nearly everyone who

lives long enough carries with it an understanding of tragedy that can be escaped only at the cost of meaning itself. Even common, human love entails suffering. If life's true griefs aren't tragic, they are meaningless, which in either case explodes any notion of a loving, heavenly Father.

So, what about tragedy, Jesus?

AN OVERNIGHT SUCCESS

IN 1958, A MIDWESTERN GIRL NAMED FRANCES MCCARTHY GRADuated as the valedictorian of her girls' prep school, Saint Alban's. Everyone in Deerfield, Michigan, thought of her as a *wunderkind*, a "golden girl," the most likely to succeed, a rising star on what could only be an ever broader horizon.

Her college and graduate school careers did not disappoint: first Princeton, then a Rhodes Scholarship, a stint at the Writer's Workshop at Iowa (for she had ambitions to write), and finally Chapel Hill, where she was awarded a Ph.D. in Comparative Literature.

At twenty-eight, she landed a tenure-track position at Barnard with a virtually guaranteed career before her.

So much had come so easily that she put off reworking her dissertation into publishable form to work on a first novel.

The novel, like most first novels, consisted of thinly-disguised autobiography, with a veneer far more revealing of Frances McCarthy's true history than her gilded public image. She wrote about herself as the thirteen-year-old daughter of a widowed prep school headmaster who is sexually preyed upon by her uncle, a history teacher on her father's faculty.

Out of pure shame, Franny, under the fictional name "Bobbie," conceals the relationship from her father. Senior boys at the school discover the uncle and the girl in bed together and begin blackmailing both: the uncle for grades and recommendations to college, the girl for sexual favors.

Not knowing how else to escape, the girl attempts suicide by taking her father's sleeping pills. Her father rushes her to the hospital in time, but during her convalescence she experiences a depression so deep she's unable to speak of her trauma. Her father decides that he cannot be the mother the girl must need at this time in her life and sends her to an all-girls school.

She performs brilliantly, out of sheer terror that she will be sent home, and graduates with all the honors the school can bestow. She alone knows the complete emotional paralysis from which she's still suffering.

Unexpectedly, publishers responded to this first novel, *Performance Anxiety*, with skepticism and even personal abuse. One of the thirty-seven rejection slips stated: "While this novel may be well written by first-time author standards, the experience of the girl is not believable. It becomes so lurid as to be absurd."

The stony response of publishers stunned Frances McCarthy. It took her a long time to recover and begin revising her dissertation into a book—an essential task, if she wanted to receive tenure and keep her job at Barnard.

Finally, her revised dissertation went into the mail and disappeared into the "slush-piles" of academic presses.

The tenure committee met. "Although given every consideration as to teaching schedule and even an entire semester to write on a college fellowship, Dr. McCarthy failed to devote timely attention to her serious research work, preferring to compose a lengthy fiction. It is the unhappy judgment of this committee that Dr. Frances McCarthy's request for tenure be denied."

Frances found a job back in Michigan at Ann Arbor. Ironically, her academic book on Goethe and Heine was published the following year, by no less prestigious a press than Yale University, and she was assured of tenure at her new university.

Franny began taking time at last for herself; she fell in love and married. David was a young Ph.D. candidate in the German department when they first met, an adjunct professor by the time they wed.

After a little more than two years, the marriage was over.

She kept the little cottage of a house she had bought before the marriage. Her car. Most everything, really.

Again a calm surface concealed a horrific undersea storm. The novel she wrote about her unhappy marriage detailed "John Caulfield's" (David's) infatuation with an older woman, "Elizabeth Whiting" (herself), and the circle she had brought him into: the moneyed classes of Grosse Pointe who ran the automobile industry. (She was surprised herself at how neatly the car business could be substituted for academia.)

The fictional John Caulfield eventually began to understand that he had been chosen because "Lizzie" believed she could dominate him. She endlessly encouraged his involvement in her rich family's affairs, urging him to accept a job with a financing corporation that her industrial power-broker father was running out of his back pocket.

John made more of a success of the financing corporation than Lizzie seemed to like. When he began to be regarded as the interesting one of the pair, she began to take them more and more out of society. Without asking John, Lizzie went to her father and asked that the business be held as a family trust. Her husband, as she had known, wanted to bring new capital to the venture. The apparent gift would keep the business small and ensure its control by its board, where Lizzie's father, his lawyer, and his banker would always outnumber John three to one.

Young John Caulfield, thwarted in his business ambitions, decided to enjoy himself, spending half his days at their country club, golfing, drinking, and sniffing out bored club women for affairs.

Lizzie repaid him in kind.

Then John fell in love again—one of his chance sexual

encounters led unexpectedly to a flourishing romance. He went to Lizzie and asked for a divorce.

The day Lizzie's lawyer served her husband with divorce papers, she released a long statement to the local gossip columnist about his many affairs.

Very quickly, John Caulfield was once again the outsider, his accounts frozen, his job gone. The woman he loved went back to her social set.

The New Model Year was published and enjoyed a brief, popular success. Critics generally commented that the author wrote too well to confine herself to soap opera.

Frances McCarthy's colleagues found her popular success distasteful. They let her know that her mercenary transformation of her troubles with young David weren't appreciated. It didn't help that the novel confessed how she had destroyed her ex-husband's life because the text implied she had successfully manipulated people in the university against David, as indeed she had.

Although Franny had tenure at Michigan, she decided to take a job in California at Berkeley. This was the 1970s. She arrived in the midst of the burgeoning women's liberation movement, when consciousness-raising groups prompted many to understand their identities in the light of sexual politics.

Franny began to conduct affairs with the private agenda of working through her early adolescent trauma. She went into psychotherapy and began to realize the murderous impulses she brought to each relationship. She stopped having affairs. She remained chaste for two years. She wrote another novel.

The book was about a serial rape victim who, twenty years after the crime, hunts down each of the perpetrators. One by one she seduces these now middle-aged men to their deaths. She asks her last victim to finish the job, to murder her. She confesses the homicidal legacy she brings to their final meeting, more interested—as a woman gone mad—in how he will respond than in her own life.

Her victim refuses. He wants only to live as "normally" as the next guy, continuing his work in real estate, behaving with his wife and children as if nothing had happened. "I'm going to forget this. I don't know you. I've never known you. I've never seen you before in my life. You've told me nothing. Nothing."

Forgetting, although highly praised by the critics, sold only 2,700 copies.

As her agent would say later, "Too dark, too true."

Frances McCarthy waited a decade—through the entire 1980s—to publish again. When she wrote another book, her old publisher not only refused it, but even admitted the firm thought she was dead.

After many rejections, *A Woman's Life* finally found a third-tier publisher.

In this novel Frances took advantage of everything she had learned to date. All the books she had written, she saw, were really one book—a story of death and the struggle to be reborn. For *A Woman's Life,* she took everything she knew about writing a growing-up story, a domestic story, and a suspense story, and she infused it all with a new appetite for hope. *A Woman's Life* came out, got good reviews, and sold as most novels do—not a lot.

Then a bankable movie star read the book, wanted to play the lead role, and managed to get the picture made. The novel's first print run of five thousand copies was succeeded by a second of 30,000, then a third of 60,000, and yet another of 100,000.

Frances McCarthy was an "overnight success."

Losses, Losses, and Then More Gains Than We'd Ever Believe

NOVELIST WALKER PERCY MADE THE COMMENT THAT WE LIVE our lives in yearning. Although counseled on every hand to "stay in the moment," the mind is predisposed to cast forward, seeking to snare the future and bring it close. That's why stories engage us, because the space between "Once upon a time . . . " and "The End" is where we live our lives. We can't help rooting for the promise of Frances McCarthy's talent to be fulfilled.

Like her, we try to anticipate difficulties. We are impelled by restlessness and anxiety toward ends that are often forgotten as soon as attained. Perhaps we love the idea of being an "overnight success" so much—and envy those we consider to be such phenomena—because they seem dispensed from having to live between the conception of their desires and the accomplishment. They don't wait. They have no need of patience. They do not yearn continually for something unrealized but instead enjoy their satisfactions and, to judge by what seem to be the prerogatives of wealth, go on enjoying them. Publications like *People* magazine make a point, in fact, of telling us how young our heroes are, as if to underline the discrepancy between the yearning-saturated life of its readers and its subjects' accomplishment in "having arrived." That's why they are the magazine's subjects and we aren't. They are the blessed; we, the benighted.

According to the parables of Jesus, though, God also yearns. God is not like an idealized movie star who has arrived at an Olympian eternity of bliss: God's personhood, his love and passion, are more akin to ours than that. God is continually moving within creation and culture and individual lives to accomplish his purposes. Often these purposes are frustrated. Sometimes horribly so. Tragically.

Before his death, Jesus himself looks over the city of Jerusalem and laments its horrible fall—a nightmare that came to pass in 70 A.D. when the Romans tried to wipe the city off the face of the earth. "Jerusalem, Jerusalem, the city that kills the prophets and stones those who are sent to it! How often have I desired to gather your children together as a hen gathers her brood under her wings, and you were not willing!"[1] Whatever we believe about Jesus' death and what he accomplished or failed to accomplish, we know that Jesus understood life's tragedy. If he were going to change history, it would not be by manufacturing it immediately to his liking.

When Jesus wants to talk about God's action in the world, his presence, he often uses the metaphor the "kingdom of heaven"—or in a closer transliteration the "reign of God." Strangely, Jesus talks about the "kingdom of heaven" or the "reign of God" without, in almost every instance, talking about a world apart from our own. Jesus tells us almost nothing about the place where the streets are paved with gold. When Jesus speaks about the kingdom of heaven, he talks about our world.

> "Listen! A sower went out to sow. And as he sowed, some seed fell on the path, and the birds came and ate it up. Other seed fell on rocky ground, where it did not have much soil, and it sprang up quickly, since it had no depth of soil. And when the sun rose, it was scorched; and since it had no root, it withered away. Other seed fell among thorns, and the thorns grew up and choked it, and it yielded no grain. Other seed fell into good soil and brought forth grain, growing up and increasing and yielding thirty and sixty and a hundredfold." And he said, "Let anyone with ears to hear listen!"[2]

Part of this parable describes just what happens when someone scatters seed on a field. Birds eat what they find, weeds compete with grains, and the quality of the soil is as important to reproductive success as the seed itself. When Jesus told this parable, people must have nodded their heads, "That's right." Then, when he got to the end, many started shaking their heads. A hundredfold? The farmers in the audience would have known that a seven percent return represented a bumper crop. A return of thirty, sixty, or one hundred percent defied agriculture at that time.

The storyteller showed his hand, his purpose, in telling the story through these last exaggerations. What did he mean?

If the kingdom of God is like the seed that's sown on the land, then it suffers losses. We might each come up with a list of things that devour, choke, or wither the presence of God in the world. Let's start with war, violence, famine, and death — the four apocalyptic horsemen. The realism or tough-mindedness of Jesus' parable has this other dimension, even when it's considered for its possible spiritual meaning. It acknowledges loss, tragedy. That is the way the world works. Jesus knows it as well as or better than anyone.

But Jesus has faith in something utterly beyond the natural — a supernatural power, the kingdom of heaven, the reign of God — that can transform the world and make it a place of abundance. He believes in heaven on earth. He believes that heaven, God's creative action within the world, will mature and grow and accomplish its purposes despite the forces that seek to destroy it. This process has already begun — God is at work in the world, as Jesus confesses through "The Sower" parable — but God will fully accomplish his purposes only in the future. In the present, God yearns to accomplish his will and invites us to join him in the process of establishing his reign.

The better-known interpretation of the parable — one attributed to Jesus himself — personalizes its terms. Those who are indifferent to Jesus' words, the seed, are the hard ground. Those who respond willingly at first and yet have no depth are like the seed that sprouts only to wither. Those who persevere for a time only to be distracted by purely worldly pleasures are like the seed that the weeds eventually choke out. Jesus' true disciples are those who receive his teaching willingly and incorporate it into their lives, becoming abundant evidence of God's love for the world itself.

There is probably a "heavenly" aspect in this speaking of heaven, too. God's love does manifest itself in the here and now, but the ultimate fulfillment of that love may have to wait until a time beyond death. If I am to believe Jesus, my grandfather's sorrow was heard—as loudly in God's ears as mine. But the conditions of this world prevented the accomplishment of that yearning until a later time.

Frances McCarthy is an image of God's reign all to herself, if also a deeply flawed and even perverse character. Her sexual innocence was violated early on—that's clear enough, even in her fictionalized retellings. She departs—wildly, it's true— from participating in the reign of God by destroying her marriage and presumably her other relationships. Yet her art becomes the vehicle by which she slowly confronts the truth of her experience and her own actions—how her anger protested against the injustice of her sexual abuse and cried out for that counterfeit of redemption: revenge. At last she comes to understand the yearning for wholeness in which she has always lived. She discerns her longing for spiritual rebirth—the hope that characterizes her last book.

I like to think that this is what enables the sum of her experience to be represented in an utterly engaging way through her last novel. All of her failure becomes enfolded into the book she has spent a lifetime learning how to write, just as what appear to be the kingdom of heaven's defeats will ultimately work to its eventual triumph.

There has to be news, of course, that Frances McCarthy hasn't discovered yet. She knows only the reality of tragedy and her own hope for spiritual rebirth. Whether that hope means anything, she cannot be sure. Only such a figure as Jesus would know, if it can be known, whether and how God intends to use all the defeats of this world for God's own victory. From the parable of "The Sower" we do know that Jesus understands tragedy and yet believes that even tragedy will be used for God's own loving and bountiful ends.

CHAPTER FOUR

WHY DOESN'T GOD SHOW HIMSELF MORE CLEARLY?

ALTHOUGH ITS VOGUE HAS NOW PASSED, I STILL REFLECT ON Samuel Beckett's seminal twentieth-century play, *Waiting For Godot*. Many of the exchanges between the principal clowns Vladimir and Estragon haunt me, none more than this:

> **Vladimir:** *We are not saints, but we have kept our appointment. How many people can boast so much?*
> **Estragon:** *Billions.*[1]

Talking about our religious searches can be wearying, because for all the talk about searching, shouldn't there be more finding? If we, like Estragon's "billions," have kept our appointment, waited at the crossroads between time and eternity, the natural and the supernatural, why doesn't God show up? Is Jesus' conception of a kingdom that knows its own seasons — suffering violence and debilities, vanquished in one place and then another before its eventual reemergence — simply an easy excuse?

We may fear that this "mystery" is only a means of manipulation.

How many "holy men" have used their "secret knowledge" as a means of scamming the gullible? "I can tell you the secret of the universe," they say, "if you'll open up your wallets."

If God's love is the "oxygen of the spiritual world," it should be readily available because we all need to breathe. If we cannot live—in any true sense—without it, the supply a merciful God keeps on hand should be unlimited. How can Jesus claim that's the case? Does he? Is Jesus sure? Why does Jesus' loving, heavenly Father seem so obvious to him and shadowy to us?

The question becomes, Why doesn't God show himself more clearly? If we all heard a voice from the sky or saw a blinding flash of light or found somehow within creation God's unmistakable signature, we would be glad to believe. But that just doesn't happen, does it? And why not?

THE GOOD POLITICIAN

Senator Goodland "Goody" Schemansky and his staff waited in their concierge-floor room while the as-yet unofficial re-election campaign's $1,000-a-plate gala in the Marriott's ballroom filled with backers whose conversations swelled with an open-bar volubility. Steven Carson, the senator's chief aide, spoke on his cell phone with another lieutenant who was monitoring the ballroom crowd. Carson wanted the meal service to follow in due time on the back of cocktails, so that alcohol and food, but not a surfeit of either, would prime his supporters for the senator's "unavoidably late arrival."

The senator could go quickly then into his speech and press the flesh afterward, when the crowd's adulation would make each personal meeting seem more than worth the price. They had TV actor Ted Franklin as emcee, and his star power would relieve any disquiet the senator's initial absence might occasion.

Marla Thorndike, the senator's publicist, sat on the suite's couch, her legs tucked to one side, as she sipped Scotch and watched the local news. The station had already shown Goody's appearance at a local day care center, and she congratulated herself on her ability to cultivate relationships as the station's sound byte included the senator's ingratiating offhand remarks with a pig-tailed three-year-old in his lap rather than his tired speech to the day care workers. Derek, the local reporter, might just be a little in love with her, she thought.

Marla flipped the channel to see if she could catch another local station's story as well.

"Look at that," Goody said. "Turn it up!"

The television showed a small car in the middle of a deserted downtown parking lot, with an army of police and medical personnel ringing the four-corner perimeter. Shots of the scenes alternated among a helicopter overview, a stationary, mid-level shot from what must have been a nearby building window, and the point-of-view camera that switched from the reporter to the strangely isolated car. Just then the helicopter shot captured a black-clad figure in a helmet approaching the car. He lingered within speaking distance for a few moments, evidently carrying on a conversation with someone inside.

"As you can see from our overhead position," the reporter said, "an officer has gone out to Peter Nunzio. We've been told that the more contact Mr. Nunzio will allow, the more he talks with police, the better chance they have of saving his life."

The man appeared to be waving something at the officer, who put up his hands as if asking the man to calm down or put away what anyone would have guessed to be a gun.

The point-of-view camera snapped off the reporter and went to close-up on the car. The man did have a gun in his hand, although now he was pointing it straight up at the roof over his head. Then he turned as if putting the gun on the seat beside him. The live feed picked up a confused shouting, and then the helicopter shot showed the officer walking slowly away from the car, back to the line of safety.

"Why didn't they rush him when he put the gun down?" Marla asked.

"As you've just seen in this ongoing dramatic confrontation, an officer of the Detroit police department ventured out to carry on a conversation with a man who has been identified as Peter Nunzio, a man who has threatened to detonate a bomb in his car, committing suicide and very possibly harming the police and medical personnel who are trying to save his life. No one knows the size of the bomb, but police reports indicate much of the Toyota Celica's back seat is stacked with a material police believe to be plastic explosive. This indicates both that Mr. Nunzio's desperate threat is no hoax and that the explosive power of the device makes this location on West Warren perhaps the most dangerous place in America at this moment."

"Peter Nunzio?" Goody asked.

Another voice broke into the report. "Donna, Donna, this is Myron Sisk in the studio again. Would you recap the story one more time for our viewers?"

"Well, Myron, as we've been reporting, Channel 9 is at a parking lot on West Warren where, since about two hours ago, a man police have identified as Peter Nunzio has been threatening to take his own life by detonating an explosive device that takes up most of the rear seat section in his Toyota Celica. About 5 P.M. tonight, Nunzio began threatening passers-by as they got into their cars for the evening commute home, bringing police here in numbers that constitute a small army. Nunzio not only allowed the parking lot to clear, but ordered police to assist this process. A number of car owners gave their keys to flak-jacketed officers, who risked their lives to drive the cars away."

"Donna, Myron again. Do we know why Peter Nunzio wants to take his own life?"

"The reports I've been getting indicate that he may be depressed over the recent break-up of his family. Mr. Nunzio is a restaurateur, although his last eatery went out of business more than a year ago. That may also have contributed."

"Peter Nunzio," Goody said again. "Steve, Steve, get off the phone for a minute. Are you watching this?"

Steve Carson lowered his cell phone for a moment and looked up.

"Nunzio worked for us, didn't he?" asked Goody. "Didn't he cater one of the neighborhood get-togethers we had during the last campaign? He makes great cannoli."

"He used to make great cannoli," Marla said.

"I remember how happy he was that day," Goody said. "He seemed to have the world by the tail."

Marla shook her head. As much as she had done to promote the idea, Goody's legendary memory for people exceeded the hype; he never forgot a name or a face or indeed anything about a constituent.

Goody went into the suite's bedroom. When he reemerged, the runty but broad-chested man was trying to get into his topcoat. "Help me with this sleeve, Marla."

Carson punched his cell phone off. "Where do you think you're going?"

"That parking lot on West Warren."

"There?" Carson pointed his phone at the screen. "You could get killed just going into that neighborhood, much less dealing with this wacko."

"Marla!"

The woman went over and helped Goody with his coat.

Carson positioned himself in front of the door.

"Look, Steve," the senator said, anticipating his aide's objections, "you've got it arranged for me to be late. I'm going to grab one of the detail officers, go over there in a cruiser, and see if there's anything I can do. I'll be back."

"What can you possibly do that the swat team can't?"

"Senator, the guy's flaked," Marla said.

"Hey people, he's one of ours."

"Because he catered an event?" Carson's face scrunched up with disbelief.

Goody gave his aide a roller-derby elbow and went out.

The police commander at the scene insisted—if the senator was really going to do this, despite his every argument—that the tuxedoed man don a flak jacket and a helmet.

After his first ten paces into no-man's land, Goody put the helmet on the ground and continued on toward the car. He saw Peter Nunzio, looking straight ahead, as if he was totally unaware of where he was and equally oblivious to the two hundred police with their guns trained on him.

"Mr. Nunzio? It's Senator Schemansky. Goody Schemansky. Remember me, Mr. Nunzio? Can I come close so we can talk?"

The man turned his head. He waved Goody over, with the gun in his hand. He poked his head out the window. "Oh, sorry, sorry. Didn't mean to . . . (he waved the gun again), I mean, I'll put the gun away. Who are you?"

Goody neared. The man's face looked waxy, struck across the nose from the street light behind them. "Peter Nunzio," Goody said. "That you? You catered one of our events two years ago. I've never had such good cannoli. You remember me, don't you?"

The man leaned out of his window to take a full look. "Holy mother, Senator, what are you doing here?"

Goody faked a laugh. "You've got all of Detroit asking that question, Mr. Nunzio. About the both of us. If you'll tell me, I'll tell you."

"You shouldn't be here, Senator. I have to . . . I have to do something. You know."

"I don't think so, Mr. Nunzio. I don't think you have to."

"Senator . . . "

"Because you see, if I weren't here, you might have to. You've got two hundred police around you. They don't really want to kill you, but a lot of weird things can happen in a situation like this—seeing as how you've put two hundred pounds of explosive in the back seat of your Toyota. But, you know, a senator's here now, a full-fledged U.S. senator, and that means some other things can happen, good things. Let me open the car door and we'll walk out of here together. The bomb guys know their job. They'll take care of the rest."

"It's really good of you to come, Senator, but I can't."

"You can't?"

"Don't you think I know, Senator, that the moment I get out of this car and start walking away, fifty cops are going to rush forward? They'll grab me up and then I'll never see you again. Not that I blame you, exactly, Senator. Not at all. But that's the reality and you know it."

"Mr. Nunzio, I keep telling you. I'm a U.S. senator. I can take you straight out of here to the hotel where I'm staying. I'll even take you to a party."

"A party?" Peter Nunzio asked. "You're crazier than me . . . if you don't mind me saying it, Senator."

"Maybe. But there is a party. I've got this big fund-raiser going on. I'm not officially running for re-election yet, but you and I both know I'm running. So the fund-raiser. Although if you tell anyone, I'll kill you."

"You'll kill *me*? How?"

They both laughed.

"Look Mr. Nunzio, Peter, I'm going to walk back to the line and tell them to clear a corridor to my cruiser. I'm going to tell them you and I are going to walk together and get into the cruiser and then I'm going to take you back to the hotel. You can even take a shower, and I'll give you some fresh clothes to wear. Then we'll both go down to the party. If I'm lying, you can tell people I've already decided to run for re-election. That'll make you a bundle from the tabloids, I bet. Come to think of it, this story will, too! It's a great story. And really a much better story if you don't blow yourself up. Far more enjoyable for the folks at the checkout lines. Okay, I'm going to walk away and then come back again for you."

Goody did as he promised Peter Nunzio. The corridor was cleared. U.S. senators can do extraordinary things.

When the senator walked back to the car, he opened the Celica's door without asking permission. He extended the man his hand. The two walked slowly toward the senator's police cruiser. Goody opened the door for his desperate guest. He went around the side of the car, cautioning the overly well intentioned to stay back. He got in beside Nunzio. "The Marriott," Goody said.

After Goody made his intentions clear to all of Detroit via the local news, his aide Steven Carson set up a big-screen TV on the dais so that the crowd could watch the senator's heroics. If he gets himself killed, Carson thought, no one will worry about the speech they missed. If he pulls it off, we'll have these people in our pockets for life!

The minute the senator got Peter Nunzio in the cruiser, the ballroom guests knew they were backing a shoo-in for re-election and ceased caring how late he was. Spontaneous dancing began.

Only thirty or so minutes later, Senator Goody appeared on the dais to applause, stamping feet, and even two-fingered whistles. Mr. Peter Nunzio appeared a moment after the senator and the clapping became lighter yet more insistent, the joyful sound of a summer shower. Goody took Peter's hand and raised both his and Peter's above their heads. "He's one of ours!" Goody shouted. "He's one of ours!"

The Thicket, the Bramble, the Desert — God's Favorite Haunts

POLITICIANS OFTEN CLAIM TO BE THE CHAMPIONS OF THE POOR and the oppressed, all the while serving their own egos. Naming a story "The Good Politician" sets us up for an ironic turn. How's the dirt going to be dished this time? Politicians provoke, at best, an ambivalent response.

Much the same would have been said about shepherds during Jesus' lifetime. Shepherding had often been used in the Judaic Scriptures as a metaphor for kingship. The tribes of Israel tell David before crowning him king: "The LORD said to you: It is you who shall be shepherd of my people Israel, you who shall be ruler over Israel."[2] In turn, David confesses that "the LORD is my shepherd."[3]

The New Testament audience knew, however, that shepherding for a livelihood meant rough, laborious, dangerous work in searing heat and freezing cold for meager rewards. Shepherds had the social status of ditch diggers. At best, several families from a village might pursue sheep herding, each household typically owning a dozen or so animals with the men sharing duties for finding pasture and water and protecting the herd from attack. Most often owners of large flocks—more than fifty—hired day laborers to tend their sheep, and these "hirelings" were famously unreliable.

Jesus uses his audience's ambivalent feelings about shepherding when he tells the story we know as "The Good Shepherd":

> Now all the tax collectors and sinners were coming near to listen to him. And the Pharisees and the scribes were grumbling and saying, "This fellow welcomes sinners and eats with them."
>
> So he told them this parable: "Which one of you, having a hundred sheep and losing one of them, does not leave the ninety-nine in the wilderness and go after the one that is lost until he finds it? When he has found it, he lays it on his shoulders and rejoices. And when he comes home, he calls together his friends and neighbors, saying to them, 'Rejoice with me, for I have found my sheep that was lost.' Just so, I tell you, there will be more joy in heaven over one sinner who repents than over ninety-nine righteous persons who need no repentance."[4]

Jesus tells this story to explain his own behavior as a reflection of heaven's or God's behavior. Why does he befriend social outcasts like tax collectors and other sinners? It's his job, he says, to go after the lost and to care for them exactly where they are, in their bewilderment and helplessness. This point depends particularly on a realistic detail: the shepherd taking the sheep on his shoulders. A sheep separated from the herd becomes pathetic and helpless and gives up—it won't go anywhere, even when prodded. It has to be carried. In the same way, Jesus will go to any lengths to find those who are lost and do whatever it takes to restore them to the company of God.

The story turns around all conventional notions of a "religious search." It's God in search of humankind, not us in search of him.

Yet Beckett's Estragon and Vladimir claim to have "kept their appointment" without any result. We may be equally convinced of the lengths people go to in their often unrewarded efforts to find God. The Westerner trekking through India into the Himalayas to find a guru and spiritual enlightenment has become a staple of the funny papers. We fill our lives with our own (economy) versions of the Tibetan trek: pilgrimages to religious sites, self-help books, conferences, adult education—all for the searching and seeking. Our common images argue that the more difficult the journey, the more arduous the task, the better our chances of spiritual success. The love of God is rare and must be pursued to the ends of the earth.

But instead Jesus teaches us of a God who pursues us, who finds us in the worst of circumstances. A God who does all the work to extract us from our willful predicaments and carry us to safety despite ourselves, where we are reunited with those whose love constitutes home.

To underline the point, the gospel of Luke places a similar story right after "The Good Shepherd." In "A Woman Who Loses a Coin," the found object—the coin—is not even animate.

"Or what woman having ten silver coins, if she loses
one of them, does not light a lamp, sweep the house,
and search carefully until she finds it? When she has
found it, she calls together her friends and neighbors,
saying, 'Rejoice with me, for I have found the coin that
I had lost.' Just so, I tell you, there is joy in the presence of the angels of God over one sinner who
repents."[5]

God pursues us, this story teaches, like a woman who
goes over every last inch of her house until she finds a coin
she knows must be there.

These stories up the ante considerably regarding God's
love. If we haven't been found by God's love, why haven't we?
When we don't feel found, we are inclined to suspect God's
nonexistence or indifference. Jesus says that can't be it at all.

Earlier, we thought of our lives as a continual door-to-door
campaign, always knocking on doors in our search for love and
acceptance and the impossible fulfillment of our deepest needs.

Jesus says, "I am the gate for the sheep. . . . I came that they
may have life, and have it abundantly. I am the good shepherd."[6]

He is the door. "Knock and it will be opened to you; seek
and you will find," he promises.

I have to consider then why I am not enjoying that love.
Why I find myself lost and helpless. Why am I not "found"?

Or perhaps I have to look at why I have never experienced
this condition of being lost. For there's an irony in Jesus' setup
to his story and its sly punch-line conclusion. "Who among you
having a hundred sheep . . . " he begins. The religious authorities
to whom Jesus spoke would have been taken aback that they could
ever consider themselves shepherds, who, despite the metaphoric
uses of the position in the Jewish Scriptures, enjoyed the status
of common laborers at best. For us this would be like starting
the story, "Who among you who is a burger flipper . . . " Even if
we thought the speaker was being facetious, we still might flinch.

When the story finishes with "there will be more rejoicing

in heaven over one sinner repenting than over ninety-nine upright people," its surface meaning seems to confirm the ninety-nine's opinion of themselves. We think we are upright and we are. As good Jews, his audience would have heard such a statement as thoroughly ironic. For clearly it's the good shepherd's action that confers blessing. Jesus was saying the religious authorities' presumption—that twinge of pride they felt on hearing themselves compared to shepherds—barred them from receiving God's blessing, which comes only to those who understand their own lost condition.

Must I then go to the ends of the earth or only to the end of my own tether to experience God's love? At the beginning of this writing I alluded to a time in my life when I asked, "Where is God?"—a time when my life made absolutely no sense and everything was crashing down.

I was in a Houston rehab center, recovering from alcoholism and tranquilizer addiction. I remember speaking with my parents during "family day." The head of the program asked all the patients and families to sit in two concentric circles facing each other—the patients in the inner circle, our families the outer. We were about to conduct an exercise called a "salad bowl." At the beginning of this exercise, the patients sat opposite their own families. Then the patients were asked to shift positions clockwise, so that we sat opposite the family of another patient. The program director asked us to introduce ourselves and tell something of what had brought us to rehab. He asked the families to share something of their stories as well. After about five minutes of discussion, the director asked the patients to shift once more, until we had spoken to all the families there and once more sat opposite our own families.

By the time we were seated again before our own families, whatever sociable veneers people brought into the room were long gone. I tried to tell my mother and father what—truly what— was bothering me. Why they found me here, in this condition, willing to sign away my own freedom as I acknowledged my sense of being utterly trapped. Emotions can be so powerful that most of us have areas we can hardly think about. If we "go there," into those memories, that room of pain, or to an outer limit before the endless space of madness begins, we fear that we will never recover. Our negative emotions threaten us with what seems like death. When I spoke to my parents on this day, I chose to go as far into these powerful feelings as I could. I'm not sure why. It's not as though I have any particular courage about such things. I'm not a brave person. Still, I chose to venture out as far as those feelings would carry me. I voiced all my pent-up resentments, fears, and anger, and tried to conjure the experience of living with these wounds. Of course I had been through almost all of this in the multiple therapy sessions that occupied our days in rehab. I think I even felt smug that I could lay out my case so well against all the ways my family had not loved me as I felt I should have been. But then, after going through more specifics than ever before, I bent over double, squeezed my eyes shut, and strangled out the sentence with which this writing began: "I feel so dead inside." This surprised my parents so much that their protests against my accusations fell away. More, far more, the sentence astonished me. That confession goes on astonishing me. The death my extreme emotions threatened turned out to be real after all; in fact, they were a form of death.

In those words I found both my death and my need of life. I found out how lost I truly was. I discovered I was in the place where Jesus says he will come to find us: the desert bramble, the empty Detroit parking lot, the moment that threatens to turn into an everlasting holocaust. That's the place where God will pick us up, put us on his shoulders, and carry us home—to a party, where there will be rejoicing. "He's one of ours!" God will say.

Jesus says that the love of God is freely available—that love searches us out. It hunts us down, even. As long as we feel we have no real need of it, though, as long as we feel safe with the flock, in whatever form that takes for us, then it's unlikely we will be picked up and rejoiced over.

Why doesn't God show himself more clearly? Jesus says, "I am the way, and the truth, and the life. No one comes to the Father except through me."[7] It strikes me that our own moments of living the truth, being in the truth, and acknowledging the same about ourselves, are rare. We need God's grace just to find the stark desert landscape of truth where God can appear to us. Jesus claims, it seems, that God's always there, searching us out, while we, in fact, don't "keep our appointments," but prefer our illusions.

This is strange enough, all by itself, to need its own explanations: Why do we prefer the comfort of our spiritual death?

SECTION II
QUARRELING

CHAPTER FIVE

WHO ARE WE?

TALK OF LOST SHEEP AND RECOVERING ALCOHOLICS AND THE woebegone as God's favorites may only lead to a common suspicion: God is for losers. God is something losers make up because they find it too hard to accept their fate. They need the comfort of this illusion.

Being a strong person, an authentic person, according to people who adopt this view, means facing a world without God and yet living according to our own principles. If these principles or ideals or purposes cannot be justified by appealing to a higher power, they still possess the meanings we ascribe to them. The world and we are worthy of love if only because we say so. God's absence provides all the more reason to embrace this life and solve its problems. We simply have to be strong enough to face a godless world, looking first to ourselves and then perhaps to others for meaning in life.

This point of view might go on to say that, unlike drunks and other losers, most normal folks know very well the truth about their lives. This notion of having to discover some dark inner secret—this journeying into a spiritual desert—in order to see God doesn't make sense. It's exactly the kind of esoteric or "hidden" teaching that religious leaders have used to manipulate people for millennia.

Jesus depicts God as the strong one, as the hero on whom we depend. My point in depicting suicidal Peter Nunzio's extreme situation was to underline this extreme lost-ness, in a way similar to Jesus' own images of lost coins and sheep.

That analogy may strike us as insulting. From one angle of vision, Jesus' parables often are. One of my favorite statements about the parables comes from John Dominic Crossan, who says the true parable often provokes hostility. "I don't know what that is," we say to ourselves on reading a parable, "but I don't like it."[1] This isn't a perverse reaction to a parable; or at least not an unexpected one. Jesus means to provoke us. Who does Jesus think we are anyway? and What does he take us for? become necessary questions.

Those are the questions, if screwed into a twisted form, that we as religious searchers are most given to ask today. Who are we? How can we discover our true identities? And, as many have suggested, is discovering our true identity the "abracadabra" of living? Another way of putting it might be: How should we account for ourselves? Do we, after all, count?

Within the context of the Gospels these questions rarely arise. Not in these forms, at least. Could it be that the absence of such self-conscious questions is as much about culture as about psychology? In first-century Judea, as in many countries today, one's self was (and is) defined by birth alone.[2]

Still, once I noticed the absence of these identity questions from the traditional literature, I rapidly became convinced that Jesus detects these questions as the true ones in the midst of conversations that seem to be about other things. He is always talking of those who have "eyes to see" and "ears to hear": who the person is becomes critical to what he can gain from Jesus' message.

Jesus does tell us who he thinks we are—or, rather, who he unfortunately knows us to be.

RICHER THAN GOD

THERE WAS ONCE A RICH MAN WHO OWNED HALF THE REAL estate in New York City, as well as casinos in Las Vegas and a transatlantic airline. His empire included cable television networks, a newspaper chain, movie studios, book publishing, and an information service. He bought fine art and wineries for diversion. Many said he was richer than God.

One night, ensconced with his girlfriend in the Presidential suite of his biggest trophy hotel, he asked the leggy blonde to read some passages from the Gideon Bible for kicks—they were that bored with each other.

"'This one thing you lack,'" the girlfriend read from the Scriptures. "'Sell all thou hast and give it to the poor and come and follow me.'"

"Stop!" screamed the rich man.

"You okay, babe?"

"What an idea!"

"Yeah, who would ever do such a thing?"

"Exactly."

Which is, initially, why the rich man set out to do just this. He no longer cared for anything his money might buy except the shock of giving it away.

He called a press conference to announce that he would be divesting himself of all his holdings.

"What plans do you have?" asked the press.

"No plans," said the rich man. "I'm just going to give it all away to the poor. The really poor."

This meant calling in all his financial advisers, who promptly informed him that he could not just *give* money away. He would have to set up a trust and let the earnings fuel his charitable projects. Do the Carnegie thing—leave a fitting legacy.

"No," he said, "that's not what it says."

"What? What says?"

"Just convert it all to cash. Cash!"

"Cash?" they asked. "You mean all of it? Liquid? That's going to take some time. We don't even really know how much you have. With the cycle we're in, you should wait . . ."

"Cash!" he screamed. (He was given to screaming.)

His girlfriend asked him that night for twenty million, if he really meant what he said.

"You're not the poor," he said.

"I've been your girlfriend for five years. If you are going to give it all away, I deserve something!"

"Sell it somewhere else, honey," he said.

She was out the door in another two minutes, leaving behind most of the expensive clothes he had bought her, but not the jewelry.

At the office the next day, his wife visited to ask, "What is this I've been reading in the papers?"

"It's true," he said.

"Then we should move on the divorce," she said.

"No," he said.

"No?"

"You're not the poor," he said.

"I will be!"

"Sorry," he said.

His two sons and a daughter by his present wife came to him. Another son by a first marriage, who was not thirty years old and a Svengali of arbitrage at Dunn & Bradstreet, approached him as well.

Then everyone who had sent him a Christmas card.

None of them was poor.

But who were the poor?

He thought of conducting a market survey. The slums would be "a target-rich environment." India a growth market. And some of those African countries nothing but. He had always known this, hadn't he?

He found this new enterprise would involve travel and

researching specifics. He had always liked hard work, though. What he hadn't reckoned on, quite, was the danger. Everyone in his life already wanted to tear him limb from limb.

The safest thing to do, he decided, was to proceed anonymously.

There was one man in all his firms whom he actually trusted, John Bieppe. An accountant with little imagination and the morals of a Puritan in a snit, John was the person he relied upon to do his own tax returns so that he wouldn't go to prison like Leona Helmsley.

"You asked for me?" John said, after he had come in.

"I'm giving all my money away. ALL OF IT!"

"You're screaming," John said.

"Sorry."

"So?"

"How should I do it? Without getting killed, I mean. Everyone thinks they're poor. Everyone!"

"You need people to help you."

"That's exactly what I don't need. All my advisers want to stay employed by putting themselves in the charity business. *Et tu*, Bieppe?"

"No, I mean, you need to give it to people who are already in the charity business. People who don't know squat about you and wouldn't care if they did."

"That sounds right. How?"

"Bieppe set him up with a charity guide, a secret and very simple office, and a good computer. He rented him a small walk-up apartment nearby, gave him the keys, and said, "Have at it!"

The rich man had about ten billion to work with (less than the sheik of Brunei's thirty-five billion than he thought) and no craving left in life except Chinese food, which he could always order in.

He started to work. At first he thought of building schools, libraries, hospitals, and the like, but then that was the Carnegie thing. *Give it away!* he thought. Really and absolutely. So he just started feeding people.

There were lots of good agencies in that business. During the next year they helped him feed a lot of people—hundreds of thousands of them—people who would have died or suffered from malnutrition.

Sometimes, though, when he stocked up an agency's food bank, the stuff was siphoned off into black markets and disappeared down someone's personal rat hole. This stung him. He wanted to start screaming again.

He was too busy to fly to these places and shake his finger in people's faces, which would not have done much good anyway. What could he do? He could stop giving the money away, but he had billions left and, if he stopped, he would have to start seeing people like his girlfriend and family again; he would rather die. The experience had changed him that much already. He liked some of these agency people with their Sears wardrobes and their foolish hopes and dreams, although they couldn't tell you where to get decent dim sum if their lives depended on it.

Because of the black market problems, he decided to send Bieppe to the heads of the agencies to inform them that if they didn't clean up their operations, their anonymous donor was going to cut them off.

Bieppe racked up a zillion frequent flyer miles putting the word out. He reported to the rich man that he kept hearing the same thing: "We'd like to. We're trying. But we don't control the world."

Well, the rich man could hire his own army and do the Western-gunslinger-at-high-noon thing, where the sad-but-true lesson about life was taught that one must stick up for what's right. This was not his way, though. He was a lover, not a fighter, except he did like to scream.

Anyway, he told Bieppe to get back to the heads of the agencies and offer new screening procedures for their personnel. He ordered psychological tests from experts.

The tests were implemented and the frequency of loss declined, but then it rose again and became even worse than it had been in the first place.

Then Bieppe, on a trip to Botswana, was killed. The locals cut off his head and mailed it to the United Nations in a UNICEF box.

The rich man truly grieved for the first time in his life. And he felt alone. His troops kept failing him in dealing with black markets. He missed Bieppe. What could he do? He still had tons and tons of money.

He would have to pursue this himself and give to anyone who cared to receive because he no longer had time to discriminate.

He called Brinks and told them to send as many trucks as were needed to the district federal depository. He ordered his banks to liquidate his remaining assets.

He set up shop in the first-floor apartment of a rundown tenement in New York's Haitian section on the upper West Side, not too far from Columbia and the Cathedral of St. John the Divine. He only had to put up a small cardboard sign outside the apartment building (as well as post two guards by the door), because once he started giving money away, the news spread fast. The police came and soon took over for the guards. The media camped out and watched. The Triboro, Verrazano, and George Washington bridges became engorged with arterial extensions of the line outside his door. New York and then the rest of the nation watched the scene develop on CNN in fascination, longing, and horror.

He gave everyone who came a million bucks. Dope pushers, socialites, pimps, Republicans, whores, con artists, Democrats, accountants, clergymen, welfare recipients: They all got a million bucks.

This worked. In four days time he gave away everything he had.

He needed to sleep after the round-the-clock marathon, and after a final press conference, in which he announced he was broke (to the media's hostile disbelief), he stumbled out of the building and realized he needed to find a place to sleep. He knew where the neighborhood soup kitchen and flop house stood; he had been funding it. He started walking.

The media was gone. All those around him were gone. He was alone. And, surprisingly, alive. For some reason, although he no longer wanted to scream, he felt terrible. He remembered the verse: "and follow me." Why hadn't anybody killed him? He found that he half longed for death because the last part was going to be so much harder.

Nothing and Everything

IN WHAT LAY THIS BILLIONAIRE'S STRENGTH? IN WHAT, HIS weakness? All I know is, I admire the guy for giving the money away. Harder than making it, I would think.

Jesus meets someone very much like my billionaire in the Gospels, a figure traditionally known as the rich young ruler. He's a princely young man who claims to have kept the commandments from his youth. An outrageous claim, as the Jews believed only Moses, Aaron, and Abraham had truly kept the Torah.

Jesus does not correct him. In fact, the gospel of Mark makes a special point in telling us Jesus loves this earnest if presumptuous young man.[3]

The rich young ruler wants to know, "What must I do to inherit eternal life?"

> Jesus, looking at him, loved him and said, "You lack
> one thing; go, sell what you own, and give the money
> to the poor, and you will have treasure in heaven; then
> come, follow me."[4]

The rich young ruler isn't up to this challenge. He goes away, grieving.

The rich young ruler has his reasons. One's obligation to

home and family in first-century Judea meant everything. The cultural obstacles to Jesus' challenge are reflected in his recitation of the commandments to the rich young ruler. The five commandments he lists (do not commit adultery, do not kill, do not steal, do not bear false witness, honor your father and mother) all specify obligations due to life and property, particularly within the context of family. For the rich young ruler, and the people of the time in general, this meant staying in the family home and seeing that its produce met the needs of parents until death.

"This one thing you lack. . . . " Jesus' lead-in makes it sound like the rich young ruler failed to keep a hidden statute; but Christ's command exposes a hidden fault line. It causes the earthquake that quickly swallows up the rich young ruler's spiritual ambitions.

To the young man's claim of righteousness, Christ as much as says, "That's fine, that's terrific, but forget it . . . forget everything you have ever based your hopes on. Abandon everything and everyone and follow me."

After the rich young ruler goes away, Jesus makes his own outrageous comment—one that has kept us sputtering ever since. "Children, how hard it is to enter the kingdom of God! It is easier for a camel to go through the eye of a needle than for someone who is rich to enter the kingdom of God."[5]

For centuries preachers have made great vats of homiletic stew over gates leading into cities or into farming estates supposedly called the Eye of the Needle. Camels are generally unburdened and crawl on their knees through these pinholes, their handlers pushing and shoving. Many analogies are then strained off.

Unlike many preachers, the disciples react without resorting to archaeology. They see such an expression as a plain impossibility. "They were greatly astounded and said to one another, 'Then who can be saved?' "

So let's restore Christ's metaphor to its full surrealism. Let's re-image this passage with him saying, "It is easier for an elephant to do the backstroke in a teacup . . . it is easier for a goldfish to play a Bach cantata . . . it is easier for a semi-trailer truck to ricochet through a microchip . . . on the natural level, it is just plain impossible!"

"The Camel and the Eye of the Needle"[6] is a riddle with a purpose rather than an answer: It's meant to provoke such frustration that we opt out of one mentality into a whole new way of looking at things.

We are all geared to "being somebody," to being respected by friends and family at the least, if not adored by the screaming rock 'n' roll fans of our daydreams. Why else would we find the promise of outward physical change so beguiling? Corporate types have a hard time disbelieving "the clothes make the man." "Makeovers" — showing a new hair color, new makeup, and a new wardrobe, with before-and-after pictures for comparison — are common fare on TV shows and in popular magazines, because who can resist becoming a "new (and substantially better) you"? People are now entranced by the computer programs plastic surgeons use to predict their patient's new appearance. The teenage obsession with tattoos and body piercing is no different; it only operates by different standards of what's desirable. All of us find ourselves seduced by the idea of improved looks or a sexier presentation.

We want a "new you," I'm suggesting, because the "old you" doesn't bring us the attention and approval we crave.

We are driven by a fundamental desire to be . . . what? What if we loved ourselves perfectly and everyone loved us perfectly and we lived in perfect circumstances? What would we be? We'd be what we, incorrectly, believe God to be. Even the existentialist philosopher Jean-Paul Sartre could see that everyone pursues the fundamental project of becoming God.

Our contemporary cult of celebrity shows us this all the time. The drive to achieve a godlike celebrity status has now proliferated or branched into "re-inventing" ourselves. If being a celebrity is good, achieving celebrity in several different guises is even better. Madonna goes from being the "material girl" to a sexual Shiva to her latest incarnation as mother and spiritual guide.

Jesus sees all this as a dodge. Do we have the courage to live absolutely for God? That's his defining question—the means by which he offers us personal definition. Who are we? We are nothing if we are not willing to be, in conventional terms, precisely nothing. He teaches that we can be authentic only by serving God in the same way that Jesus serves the Father. This is the way to have eternal life, the life of God within us, in this life and the next.

Whatever else following Jesus may be, it's not for the timid. The very beginning of the way Jesus offers to us demands everything.

Then it gets harder. For we can no longer rely on our true crutches—the approval of others, wielding power, social standing, prestige, wealth—none of it. Jesus asks us to take the ultimate risk. If we risk all he promises,

> "In truth I tell you, there is no one who has left house,
> brothers, sisters, mother, father, children or land for
> my sake and for the sake of the gospel who will not
> receive a hundred times as much, houses, brothers,
> sisters, mothers, children and land—and persecutions
> too—now in this present time and, in the world to
> come, eternal life. Many who are first will be last,
> and the last, first."[7]

In "Richer Than God" my Trump-like billionaire takes the challenge that the rich young ruler refuses. He accepts the challenge that the disciples, after deserting Jesus at the cross, must return to. My billionaire finds the rewards that Jesus promises, too, as his sheer obedience, even though prompted by little more than boredom, carries him into participating in the reign of God. We are such materialists these days that his action may astound us; it may seem the height of Christian virtue. But what Jesus teaches the disciples is that absolute commitment and obedience in that commitment is the *beginning* of following his way. We get what we want only by abandoning everything, even our very selves. "For those who want to save their life will lose it, and those who lose their life for my sake, will save it. What does it profit them if they gain the whole world, but lose or forfeit themselves?"[8] Jesus tells us we can find ourselves only by serving God until death—be it as martyrs or as old people expiring in our sleep. He asks us to accept the poverty of the Son of Man, who had no place to lay his head, for a reward that exists as a present mystery and future promise. We ask, Who are we? Jesus responds, "Follow me and I will show you."

What then is my billionaire shown? First, the emptiness of a life lived to please oneself. The attempt to make ourselves into God, however outwardly successful, produces what the philosopher Kierkegaard called the "sickness unto death." We are not the kind of creatures who can invent our own values, pursue them, and find ourselves satisfied. It doesn't work. We begin to grasp life, real life, only when we put our lives at God's disposal. This involves giving up things that aren't easy to give up, a process of renunciation that can take a long time to convince us that the regard of others doesn't matter. But gradually, like my billionaire, we may find ourselves in a new element, surrounded by people who are filled with purpose rather than envy and insatiable appetite, aware of struggles and needs that are so much greater than our own. And if God leads us this far, as God has my billionaire, then God, according to Jesus, will also supply the true reward of a restored life, in this world and in the world to come. We won't lose out in the only evaluation that counts.

But, again, is this what we want?

CHAPTER SIX

HOW CAN WE BE TRULY FREE?

As much as we admire the Mother Teresas of the world or romanticize the Orthodox monks on Mt. Athos living lives exclusively devoted to contemplation or—closer to home—wonder about the spinsterish existence of a single, Protestant woman who pours out her life working with the elderly, do we really want to live that way?

Hardly. We want to be free, to define our lives as much as possible through pure choice. Isn't this the entire reason for striving after political freedom? The right to pursue happiness as we conceive it?

As Cardinal Newman writes, even most religious people are simply interested in how much they can live for themselves without offending God.[1]

The temper of the times and our therapeutic society put us at odds with the notion that freedom consists of following someone else.

If we admit that as creatures our freedom can be limited by our environments or circumstances, we direct our efforts to improving these circumstances in order to maximize our freedom. We work at our relationships, careers, child-rearing techniques, exercise programs, and every other aspect of our lives to construct personal spaces that gratify our expectations. We will be happy, we tell ourselves, when we lose ten pounds, communicate more effectively with our significant other (increasing sexual pleasure in the bargain), employ parenting strategies that keep our kids on track to college and their own successful futures, and win the approval of superiors and coworkers and the financial rewards that go with it.

On the flip side of this same equation, we will be happy when our emotional lives are freed from the past's netting. If we suffer from dysfunctional families or the wounds of past disappointments and bad relationships, then we must free ourselves by identifying how we have tied ourselves into emotional knots and sundering these through positive action. The mind itself possesses an inherent drive toward emotional wholeness that will triumph given enough therapeutic support. This is self-validation, not renunciation. As the current Hollywood phrase goes, "You have to stamp your own passport."

We are the self-created; both the technical prowess and the psychological sophistication of the West, which have so dramatically affected our outward and inward environments, promise this is the way to go. So we are always reaching, reaching, reaching for that brass ring.

It's easy to represent these developments in such airy ways that they deflate as easily as soufflés. But give them their due. Scientists point out that any organism—the lowliest clam—tries to affect its environment for the better. People do the same and it would be a sorry world if they didn't. A religious view cannot afford to neglect the value of human effort or the dignity of work—or the relation between circumstance and well-being.

Likewise, the mind does seem to have its own curative properties. Good counsel and friendship, under whatever auspices, professional or otherwise, truly help many people achieve a never-before-experienced emotional freedom.

We like to feel good. Is that wrong? Why does Jesus insist on self-denial, not validation, as the way to be free?

FLIP-FLOPS

SALLY ENTWHISTLE BOARDED A CESSNA 180 FLOAT PLANE FOR
the run west of Tahiti to the island Lanie Lanea to attend her
sister's funeral. Sally had not seen her sister in a dozen years,
not since their father died and ninety percent of his estate went
to Lanie. She hadn't even known where her sister was. The
summoning call informed her that Lanie owned a tropical
island, and that for the past two years she had lived there with
her money manager, Barry. She died in a boating accident,
along with her two closest friends, fellow Smith College alumna.

The service proved embarrassingly minimal. The Methodist
minister who flew in with her stood at the edge of the island's
western headland. Barry and Sally were the only other
mourners — relatives of the friends who had died with Lanie
asked that their remains be returned to the States. Only the
hulk of the exploded yacht in the harbor and the charred ground
back of the house where Dukey the butler had cremated Lanie's
body spoke of the tragedy.

When the minister asked, neither Barry nor Sally had anything to say by way of eulogy. He read a few things from his
small black prayer book, and then he asked — insisted,
actually — that Sally dump the urn's contents over the headland's
edge. Luckily, there was an offshore wind, and the ashes plumed
out over the broad, turquoise sea.

"Let's go back to the house and all have a drink together,"
Sally said.

"You won't shake it there," Barry said.

"Shake what?"

"I suggest we go to my house. Much more comfortable."

"Your house?"

"That little gate house. You probably noticed it on your way in. That's where I've been putting up my flip-flops. You won't shake what you're feeling in the Big House. The Big House *is* what you're feeling."

Sally looked at the minister, questioning how a money manager could become so mysterious.

"The plane's due back at six. I'm not even to spend the night," the minister said, inviting the two others into his surprise and resentment at such treatment.

"I'm sorry," Barry said. "She didn't want a minister here for long."

"I'll be on a plane thirty-six hours here and back," the minister said, begging understanding.

They walked onto the graded road between the harbor and the mansion. "Reverend, we have some business. Why don't you go up to the house and rest while you have a chance? I'm sorry not to be friendlier. I guess we've lost the habit here. Dukey will give you a massage if you like. Work out the kinks before your travel starts again."

The minister looked at Barry, his consternation bleaching his lips. Then he glared at the deceased's sister. "I'm sorry for your loss . . . Sally," he said, and put out his hand awkwardly. "I wish I could have been of some comfort, but then people have to grieve to feel the need of it." He turned smartly and walked away.

Sally wasn't at all sure she wanted to go down to Barry's gate house.

"If you're wondering, there's no will to read," Barry said. "Lanie died intestate. But I have some things to tell you — what you'll need to know."

The gate house, like the Big House, was stone, Louis XIV, with its own tympanum and columned entrance, a high mansard slate roof, huge front palladium windows, and multiple sets of double doors at the back that led out into the inescapable tropical garden. Sally thought about the expense of building a knock-off Versailles here. And how? It would have taken shiploads of men and material and demanded they live for

years in provisional camps. She wondered if there were pictures—the first time anything about Lanie Lanea made her
feel curious rather than queer.

Barry led Sally out back to the loggia and brought her an
old-fashioned glass of single-malt Scotch—Glen Fiddich, she
guessed.

"It's all mine," she told Barry straight off. "Whether she died
with or without a will, it's all mine. Though I have to tell you,
for paradise, this place gives me the creeps." She paused. "Of
course you give me the creeps, too, Barry. I've always been
forthright about that." She smiled and sipped.

"I knew you'd come here to say as much. But what exactly
do you think is yours?"

"All of it," she said. "Everything my father left and what Lanie
did with it the last twelve years. She may have been able to escape
the courts, but evidently justice caught up with her, didn't it?"

"You may be right about that," he said. He sipped his drink.
"What Lanie 'did with it' may prove impossible to determine,
Sally—that's what I have to tell you. In fact, I'm certain of it."

Sally stood up. "I'm not going to sit here and have you tell
me how you are going to steal it all away from me one more
time. I'll have you bombed off this tropical atoll before I'll let
that happen."

"Sit down, sit down," he said. "I have no use for your
money." The strange fatigue that came over him, a depression
she had sensed ever since he helped her out of the float plane,
convinced her.

He didn't look at her but out at the line of palms beyond the
scruffy-grassed formal garden as he said, "I was going to leave. I
moved into the gate house as soon as it was habitable. Your sister
started pushing me away right after we arrived. It was all the
money—it always was. She knew that there's nothing more
common than a man stealing a woman blind. I might have. Probably
would have in the early going if I had been more ambitious. But
there was just so much money. Who needed to steal?"

"You both did a nice enough job of it when it came to me."

"Your father composed his own will."

"Thirty-six times!"

Barry shrugged. "He was your father. Anyway, your two marriages set you up. I could never understand why you wanted to spend your ex-husbands' money on lawyers."

"That was just it—my ex-husbands' money. I wanted my own family's money."

"So how much do you think is left?" Barry asked.

"Lanie was many things, but she was prudent about money. I imagine the estate's grown."

"Too prudent. Your sister kept devising ways to make the money more difficult to get at. She thought anonymous Swiss bank accounts were about as safe as a 7-Eleven cash drawer. She devised a code for her code numbers, and then distributed parts of it to her late friends and to me. She alone knew everything about everything. Among the three of us, the Smith College sisters and I, we would have known everything, too, if we had been able to compare notes."

"We were going to," Barry admitted. "Right after your sister gave out the code pieces at our yearly get-together. Unfortunately, your sister discovered some of my communications to Edith and Margo. I guess she decided to put the expression 'you can't take it with you' to the test."

"She killed herself? She killed Edith and Margo?"

"Why else would a sixty-foot yacht blow up in the middle of a tropical harbor on a cloudless day?" Barry took a long sip of his Scotch. "I'm sure she meant to get off in time. The butler, Dukey, must know what went wrong, but Dukey's not talking. I have no doubt she meant to murder her friends. The point is, the only use she had for people was to import them for parties. She talked all day long about hating Edith and Margo, and everybody else, for that matter."

Barry rubbed his whiskered chin and squinted up into the sun. "It's been my privilege in this life to watch vast wealth reduce a woman to being a prisoner in her own Big House. 'No man is an island,' to quote Donne. She was more like a volcano.

What a mouth that woman had. No one wanted to play amidst her lava fields for long."

"Well, there are records," Sally said. "Even erasures from a computer's hard disks are recoverable. We can follow whatever trail exists and force the bankers to give up her assets."

"Are you hearing me?" Barry asked. "You're already rich. How rich do you have to be?"

"But it would be imprudent of me to let the money languish in dead accounts."

"'Dead accounts.' Now there's a poetic phrase. Better than Donne."

"What are you talking about?" Sally asked. "I can see why Lanie came to hate you. Isn't that something. Finally, in death, she and I agree on something."

"Yes, you do."

Not Knowing When We're Well Off

THE COUNTERPOINT TO WHAT THE PSYCHIATRIST PHILLIP RIEFF has called the "triumph of the therapeutic" in our society must be Howard Hughes starving to death as a drug addict in his own penthouse suite. Doris Duke becomes the patsy of the last people who could stand being around her. The King himself, Elvis, slumps to the ground from a porcelain throne, his mind as befouled as his intestines by drugs. Why do those who "have it all" so often become their own victims, ending their lives as isolated and often hateful people?

We think of such examples as curiosities, so extreme both in blessing and curse that they don't serve as cases in point of anything. They certainly have nothing to do with us, we think. There's probably no lesson to be learned here, other than you *can* be too rich and even, in Howard Hughes's case, too thin.

Jesus connected his own story of a Howard Hughes to what appears to be a universal and laudable human impulse—the desire for justice. Jesus' story is prompted by someone who feels his rights are being violated. A man who, like the younger sister Sally in "Flip-Flops," believes he's been unjustly denied a portion of a family inheritance. Jesus' parable quickly shifts from a consideration of justice to our motivations in seeking it.

> Someone in the crowd said to him, "Teacher, tell my brother to divide the family inheritance with me." But he said to him, "Friend, who set me to be a judge or arbitrator over you?" And he said to them, "Take care! Be on your guard against all kinds of greed; for one's life does not consist in the abundance of possessions." Then he told them a parable: "The land of a rich man produced abundantly. And he thought to himself, 'What should I do, for I have no place to store my crops?' Then he said, 'I will do this: I will pull down my barns and build larger ones, and there I will store all my grain and my goods. And I will say to my soul, 'Soul, you have ample goods laid up for many years; relax, eat, drink, be merry.' But God said to him, 'You fool! This very night your life is being demanded of you. And the things you have prepared, whose will they be?' So it is with those who store up treasures for themselves but are not rich toward God."
>
> He said to his disciples, "Therefore I tell you, do not worry about your life. . . . "[2]

Jesus responds to the impromptu demand by questioning his petitioner's motives. Does the man really want justice or is he simply greedy? The petitioner presumes that Jesus will side with him in the dispute—he may be seeking to use Jesus' stature as a religious teacher to sway the outcome of the case. Jesus has no interest in using his influence in this way. The petitioner's presumption accounts for the curtness of Jesus' reply ("Friend, who set me to be a judge or arbitrator over you?"). The parable then elaborates on human presumption itself, which involves not only the question of justice, as we'll see, but also how our attitudes toward justice reflect the freedom or bondage of our souls.

Like Jesus' other stories, the parable of "the rich man" contains so much in such a brief space that we have to meditate on each line, each phrase, each word to understand its full implications. Right at the beginning we have to slow down enough to understand the implications of the rich man's perception of the land's bountiful harvest as a problem. "What am I to do?" he asks. This captures his mentality. While we may draw the inference later that he is pleased by the harvest, he is certainly not grateful for it. He does not perceive it as God's gift but as his problem.

Jesus speaks the parable, of course, within the context of a religion that identified an abundance of material goods with God's blessing. We think of Joseph serving as Pharaoh's steward over the years of plenty in preparation for the time of famine. Joseph then becomes the savior of his traitorous family, which reveals the hidden purposes of God. We also think of the Lord himself providing manna to the Israelites in their wanderings through the desert. We think of the psalmist who writes of the Lord preparing his table in the presence of enemies.

But the rich man thinks of none of this. Unlike Joseph, he sees himself not as a steward of God's bounty but as the creator of a self-enclosed world—as a "self-made man," who is arranging his environment. Stamping his own passport. So he has a problem, not an opportunity. He thinks—or presumes—he is in control.

The harvest is so great that his present barns will not house it. We must suppose that these are ample to his own needs and the needs of his family. After all, he is already a rich man, and the text underlines this in the original by the slight redundancy of calling him a rich man who owned a great deal of land. (At the time, there was no other way to be rich.) Yet he never thinks of the storage, as Helmet Thielicke says, that might be provided by the mouths of the poor. He never even consults with anyone else about his "problem." He is alone with his thoughts.

Whatever his supposed beliefs, the rich man lives as an atheist. Indeed, as the god of his own world. The story emphasizes this in several ways. The third person "There was once a rich man" narration gives way to the character's own soliloquy, which carries the story until God's direct intervention. The rich man's selfishness comes through in the possessives, "my barns," "my grain," "my goods," and finally "my soul." He believes he owns himself—that it's his life.

Almost everyone would claim such ownership today. The play *Whose Life Is It Anyway?* asks what has become a rhetorical question; we immediately think, Mine! We have to pause to realize that the entire Judeo-Christian tradition gives a wholly different answer; it maintains we are stewards of our own lives. Today we are so preoccupied with self-determination, maintaining control, and refusing to be victims that we lack any sense of our lives as gifts.

When the rich man's presumption reaches its height, Jesus quotes God as thundering, "Fool!" Elsewhere Jesus counsels us to call no man fool. God alone can make such a judgment. God does so here because the rich man's attitudes, we can only guess, qualify him as the psalmist's "fool," who says in his heart that there is no God. When he says, "my soul," he certainly presumes as much. The rich man is the Epicurean of the time, who believed, as St. Paul writes elsewhere, in eating, drinking, and making merry, for tomorrow, when death comes, death will be the end. Death is not an end, however, but another beginning.

Reality breaks through to the rich man in the summons to his death. The Lord has given him his life and now requires him to make an accounting of it. At the worst possible time. Whose goods will the bountiful harvest be now? Others, for whom God intended them. And the rich man must go to his death with no treasure in heaven because he has never built a storehouse there.

If there is no God and we will never be summoned to such an accounting, then putting windfall profits into new barns or inheritances into secret-coded bank accounts in order to live the good life represent reasonable choices. But there's this curious anomaly: When a person manipulates circumstances to gratify his or her own desires, to the point of using justice or status as a pretext, the person inevitably becomes miserable. Those who hold to no spiritual view of life at all can observe that something on the order of "spiritual death" afflicts the greedy. Aristotle remarked that the surest way to destroy someone was to give the person his own way.

The success and therapeutic models of the good life in our time presume that people themselves know what's in their own best interest. Both models concern themselves with providing techniques for the acquisition of self-discovered ends: what we decide we want. But what if we don't know what we want? Worse, what if our natural desires ultimately run counter to our own good? We may not even know what we should want.

What if our true and best life is "hidden" in God and only God can reveal that life to us? Then our techniques for successful living are to no avail.

In my own life I tried to do something very much like Jesus' petitioner did. I tried to use Jesus' influence to ratify my own choices. I'm one of those fortunate people who understood not too long after childhood where his gifts lay. I knew I'd have to be a writer and teacher or pretty much nothing because I loved stories and could answer the teacher's questions about them, whereas in other things my talents were thoroughly ordinary. I had one gift to cultivate.

Like the rich man or Lanie Entwhistle, I perceived my gift as a problem as much as anything else. How would I use it?

How could it best bring me the status and financial rewards and relationships that I craved? Freud let everyone know that writers are interested in using their talents for money and sex—whatever their pretensions. I'd have to confess he had my number.

At the same time, I thought of myself as a Christian and so I wanted God's blessing on my plans. I didn't invite God to make these plans, of course. Not seriously. My prayers were on the order of "you want me to do this, right?"

I never stopped to consider the possibility that the gift might be God's, not mine. That I was to be its steward, using it for God's purposes. I remember the first time my psychiatrist remarked that a book I was working on might be tremendously useful to other people. The idea shocked me. Its usefulness had nothing to do with my motivation for writing it. Its only "use," as I conceived it, would be to redound to my greater glory. (Unfortunately most writers in our time operate on the same principle. They often represent this as humility—they would never presume to influence others for the good, only to entertain them or give them information.) Clearly, I had no idea how to conceive of the "good life" past my own selfish interests.

My use of God's gift for my own ends eventually made me miserable. I was pretending to be something I wasn't—a great rather than modestly gifted writer. I went so far as to pretend that God endorsed my pretensions.

I finally began to find comfort in my vocation only when I put it at God's disposal. Daily I pray that God will show me what to do just as God likes—for I know that God's will being done on earth as it is in heaven means my true happiness.

Similarly, perhaps the most famous conversion in history, next to St. Paul's, occurred when St. Augustine reached the end of his own "gifted tether." A fourth-century orator and teacher of rhetoric, who was on track to become the Roman emperor's chief advisor, Augustine came down with career-threatening laryngitis. He lost his voice. The strain of his ambitions seems to have resulted in what were psychosomatic symptoms—at least a close reading of his *Confessions* leads me to suspect this. For after Augustine gave his happiness into God's hands, he recovered his voice and went on to become the emperor's chief advisor, without any sense of strain. Augustine's sense of God's appointment allowed him to do easily what he could not do by himself.

The parable of the rich man suggests this is a common, even universal, human experience. We all have something we want to horde—money, our personal gifts, or simply our freedom itself, not allowing anyone to brook our hallowed, self-validating choices. Few people of mature reflection will not see all the trouble this has caused in their lives. It's a lesson that can be tragic in the learning. We all have to serve somebody; and if we choose ourselves for masters, we are in for quite a beating.

After speaking the parable, Jesus orders us not to worry about even basic needs: what we eat, how we clothe our bodies. This is often regarded as friendly and rather touching advice. It's not. It's an order. Following in the way of Jesus means this: "You must not set your hearts on things to eat and drink; nor must you worry." We must not. We are to think only of how to participate in the reign of the kingdom and leave all our needs to God. Because God alone understands what's good for us.

Our pride and ego take us away from this good into unreality. They foster spiritual illusions that are spiritually deadly.

Perhaps we have such a difficult time believing in a generous heavenly Father because we do not want one. We want to control our own lives. We want justice conceived in our terms. We want to be free to do just as we please. We want to have it all!

Jesus is telling us that we do have it all when the all is Jesus himself. True freedom means following Jesus in seeking after the kingdom of God.

Do not worry about your life, Jesus says, give it to me. You can count on God's love for everything from daily needs to the fulfillment of personal destiny. What greater freedom could there be?

CHAPTER SEVEN

IS GOD FAIR?

WHAT JESUS TEACHES GOES AGAINST THE GRAIN. HOW MANY, I wonder, find it attractive? We can have the love that lies at the heart of the universe within our own lives, but we have to let that love have its way, to the point of re-creating who we are. We are invited to allow God to do this, not, curiously enough, to do it ourselves. Considered as a self-help manual, Jesus' parables suggest there's no helping the self—the self cannot help itself because it's blind to its own good, the slave of appetites and the stooge of a perverse ego. We are asked to opt for another way of becoming our true selves, a way of imitation, patterning our lives after Jesus' own obedience to God.

As the last two chapters explain, we can find our true identities only by renouncing our own wishes; we can only be truly free if we follow Jesus in seeking after the kingdom.

It has to be admitted that something in us really hates this. We like helping ourselves. Everyday experience teaches that life is about problem solving. But in effect we are saying, Jesus went to a lot of trouble to point out there's a problem the human person simply cannot solve. And that problem is the way we are. We don't know what's good for us.

Wasn't it pointed out previously, however, that the witness of conscience within us does guide us? In the very first story, "The Corvair at Midnight," we found within ourselves a voice that demanded the destitute family be received. In "The Friend at Midnight" Jesus himself affirmed at least the concept of human shame. So Jesus seems to be arguing both ends against the middle; we know there must be a God because every one of us lives in a moral universe, which would be senseless if God did not exist. Yet, although we understand the difference between right and wrong, we cannot choose the good for ourselves—we are blind to our own good. How can both be true?

Maybe our sense of right and wrong and our own choices are not in such dramatic conflict. Maybe Jesus isn't being fair to who we are. If this is what Jesus thought about human nature, his understanding of God may lack an essential fairness—we are not *that* bad. Or I might be overemphasizing his negative statements at the expense of his encouraging advice—for example, love your enemies—where Jesus seems to presume that the individual can choose the good. Representing Jesus' views in the way I have almost makes it seem as if there's no point in being a spiritual seeker—why strive after the unattainable?

Also, if we constitute our own dilemmas, if we are the problem, we must be absolutely at God's mercy. Again, that doesn't seem fair because there are worlds of differences, to our eyes, between serial killers and the reliable neighbor two doors down who lets us borrow his Weed Eater or our girlfriend who will always speak up for us even if it makes her unpopular. We know something about common human virtue; it's not unreal.

We have developed two different objections to Jesus' view of human nature. I'd like to personify these objections by introducing two different contemporary questioners. The first would be a spiritual seeker—in fact a spiritual athlete. What if a seeker asked Jesus to give her a program—a "course of miracles"—that would enable the seeker to achieve spiritual enlightenment? Someone who, unlike the rich young ruler, was truly willing to do whatever it took—chastity, ascetical exercises, vegetarianism, the works? What would Jesus have said to this Alice the Spiritual Athlete?

Also, let's imagine someone who has a fair amount of common sense, who proposes that a life of common triumph and defeat shouldn't be nay said. A Johnny Lunch Pail might ask Jesus to consider whether good, honest, hard-working people aren't really the salt of the earth. That fundamentally people are good, and they choose to do good more often than they choose to do bad. Their choices might not always be perfect, but they do know how to get along in this world. There are lots of people we might imitate whose lives depend mostly on common wit and wisdom.

Did Jesus have questioners of either ilk? Did any Alices or Johnnys appear? What did he make of some people's capacity for self-improvement and their native understanding of getting along?

THE INVISIBLE HAND OF
THE MARKETPLACE

IN THE MID-1970S A NEW BANK DIRECTOR CAME TO PACIFIC Western. He made himself the mortgage loan officer for a lower-middle-class Latino and Asian neighborhood on the border of the South Central projects in Los Angeles. This neighborhood had been red-lined for years, with lending formulas that made it much more difficult for its residents to buy properties than for average suburbanites.

After the inflationary year of the Gulf embargo, interest rates eased, and the director made use of adjustable rate mortgages (ARMS) to get people into houses. Instead of turning people away, the bank began approving loan applications. The director even visited community groups to let people know they might qualify. Shopkeepers, civil servants, teachers, and machinists who worked at Hughes Aircraft and Lockheed became homeowners for the first time. Block parties busted out like so many hosannas.

Then, in the days of President Jimmy Carter, stagflation set in, the country found itself in a "malaise," and, more significantly for this particular community, crack cocaine lit a butane fire under the violent drug trade. Those who could moved, and those who couldn't — or many of them — struggled. The three-year review period of the ARMS came up, and the interest rates rose the two points allowed for by their terms.

The bank director came to spend much of his time with people at risk of defaulting on their loans. The bank was in no trouble, as it had good cash reserves. The hike in interest rates allowed for many safe investments with a high rate of return, consumer loans were lucrative, and Visa card rates were truly phenomenal. So the bank director examined carefully the cases of those in jeopardy of default. For some he retracted the hike in interest rates; for others he provided relief for a specified time that would see them out of the stagflationary period; and in a few instances he forgave the entirety of the mortgage altogether.

This time private celebrations were held. Still, word got out.

Those who had not had their loans renegotiated came to the bank director and said, "How can you do this? We are slaving to pay your 16 percent and here you go and cancel other people's debts. We'd like our debts canceled, too!"

"Hey, you agreed to the terms of the loans," the bank director said.

"Sure we did, but . . . "

"You were glad enough to get those loans before."

"We can't believe this. It's so unfair."

"Look. It's more important for your community to have

conscientious homeowners than anything else right now. Do
you want to destroy the neighborhood and see your own homes
depreciate?"

"What we want is justice!"

Wanting Justice

IN RESPONSE TO "THE INVISIBLE HAND," SOME MAY BE THINKING:
Here we go; we start off talking about conscience, spiritual dedi-
cation, and common sense, but we quickly spin into a socialist
bromide. Others may feel gratified, even taken off the hook: Jesus
as the friend of the poor. The exploiters versus the compassionate.
That's a dichotomy that allows those of small means to place
themselves easily among the righteous. But, for starters, how
comfortable would we have felt if we had been among the hard-
working poor whose loan payments were not lowered or forgiven?
I'm trying to angle in here at something that applies to all of us,
rich and poor, free marketers and welfare-staters alike.

Money is the most valuable metaphoric coin for the job.
Jesus' parables talk about money almost constantly. From
the famous "Prodigal Son" to "The Lost Coin" and on to the
parabolic episode of Peter and Jesus paying their taxes from
the mouth of a fish,[1] Jesus uses money to reveal who we are
and what we want. His stories about money show us the way
our world works and how God realizes his presence within
our world.

Moreover, Jesus used assets in his stories—not just money,
but sheep, land, grain, and even social status and religious
standing—to show the things we care about. Particularly in
the Sermon on the Mount,[2] Jesus provides his own "economy"
of life, transforming our conception of what's an asset and
what's not.

Jesus' storytelling hits us where we live. "For where your treasure is, there your heart will be also," he tells us.[3] Jesus makes the pairing of treasure and the heart a primary theme. What do we want? Well, what are we spending our money on?

"The Invisible Hand of the Marketplace" takes its inspiration from Jesus' parable "The Laborers in the Vineyard." Both are about money. Both should make us uncomfortable. In fact, Jesus' parable has been striking its hearers as unfair for two thousand years. In Matthew's account Jesus tells the parable in explanation of his dealings with the rich young ruler. Jesus has just pointed out how hard it is for a rich man to enter the kingdom of heaven and goes on to promise that those who forsake all for his sake will be richly rewarded one day. He goes on to explain these "reversals of fortune" through another parable.

"For the kingdom of heaven is like a landowner who went out early in the morning to hire laborers for his vineyard. After agreeing with the laborers for the usual daily wage, he sent them into his vineyard. When he went out about nine o'clock, he saw others standing idle in the marketplace; and he said to them, 'You also go into the vineyard, and I will pay you whatever is right.' So they went. When he went out again about noon and about three o'clock, he did the same. And about five o'clock he went out and found others standing around; and he said to them, 'Why are you standing here idle all day?' They said to him, 'Because no one has hired us.' He said to them, 'You also go into the vineyard.' When evening came, the owner of the vineyard said to his manager, 'Call the laborers and give them their pay, beginning with the last and then going to the first.' When those hired about five o'clock came, each of them received the usual daily wage. Now when the first came, they thought they would receive more; but each of them also received the usual daily wage. And when they

received it, they grumbled against the landowner, saying,
'These last worked only one hour, and you have made
them equal to us who have borne the burden of the day
and the scorching heat.' But he replied to one of them,
'Friend, I am doing you no wrong; did you not agree
with me for the usual daily wage? Take what belongs to
you and go; I choose to give to this last the same as I give
to you. Am I not allowed to do what I choose with what
belongs to me? Or are you envious because I am generous?' So the last will be first, and the first will be last."[4]

Any worthwhile understanding of this parable begins by reg-
istering the shock of the landowner's paying all his workers
equally. If the reader is like me, he doesn't like this. My sym-
pathies are with the grumbling workers.

This puts me on the spot because, according to Matthew,
Jesus begins this parable for his disciples by identifying the
parable as an extended metaphor or comparison, "The kingdom of heaven is like . . ."

Is the kingdom like the sentiments expressed by the grumbling
workers? Mine are. Doesn't this kingdom have an instinctive sense
of fairness or equity? Or is my sense of justice too limited? Once
again, is God fair?

Many commentators have seen "The Laborers in the Vineyard" as expressing the logic of grace, as opposed to the logic of
merit. That is, God responds to us, as the landowner does to the
late-arriving workers, in terms of what we need, not what we
deserve. The late-arriving workers and their families need as
much money as the first-arriving to survive for any length of time.
The wealthy landowner supplies this, and in so doing alleviates
the hardship of changing economic times. He exemplifies mercy.

The landowner also extends the invitation personally. In
this aspect the story departs strikingly from realism, as a
wealthy landowner's steward would have done such hiring.
The landowner's personal and repeated invitation identifies
him with Jesus and his invitation to everyone to come into the

kingdom. Once there (in the vineyard, in the kingdom), Jesus treats everyone equally, if individually. The kingdom seems to know nothing of the usual pecking orders.

As I've thought about this parable, its key moment has become the landowner's direct address to one of the grumbling workers.

> "Friend, I am doing you no wrong; did you not agree with me for the usual daily wage? Take what belongs to you and go; I choose to give to this last the same as I give to you.
>
> "Am I not allowed to do what I choose with what belongs to me? Or are you envious because I am generous?"

Our bank officer says essentially the same to the complaining homeowners. Jesus' laborers and the homeowners want to make not only their reward but in fact anyone's reward or punishment absolutely contingent upon service. They want to confine justice to quid pro quo: this reward or honor or punishment for that action. This results in the mistaken notion that we're talking about justice, when we're not. We talk ourselves into forgetting the deals we've made, while concealing our resentment of those who receive mercy.

The laborers refuse to rejoice in the landowner's merciful actions, and the landowner faces them down and sends them away, which strongly implies Jesus' own judgment against those who would do the same. Anyone, Jesus seems to be saying, who wants to make reward absolutely contingent upon service doesn't understand how God works. The desire to dictate terms to God can actually pit us against him.

This applies to both Alice the Spiritual Athlete and Johnny Lunch Pail because it addresses ever more closely the corruption of human conscience. In many instances we may know the difference between right and wrong, but there's a dark irony: We use this sense in order to exalt ourselves at the expense of others. The spiritually dedicated may want the knowledge of God to be hard to come by—may even insist upon it. The hard-working, common-sensical person may see his or her own efforts devalued by any show of mercy. We are so anxious for justice that we become the enemies of grace.

Although allegorical interpretations of the parables are in disfavor, it's hard to resist the notion that Jesus tells "The Laborers in the Vineyard" story partly to refute the Jewish religious authorities, the Pharisees, who elaborated the written Torah to such a degree that the poor were excluded in practice from God's mercy. They bear a striking resemblance to the "first-hired," particularly as a "vineyard" is a common motif for Israel.[5] The Pharisees were the spiritual athletes of the day—our Alices—and wanted to keep spiritual reward for those who, like themselves, could expend the necessary effort.

The workers hired later in the day, who do not come to an explicit bargain with the vineyard owner but agree to "what's right," can well be thought of as the common man or woman whose "common sense" of justice would argue against divine mercy. Those whose good sense—our Johnny Lunch Pails—conceals the desire to be thought better than the next guy. And who among us has no desire for reputation? Can anyone say he or she has never desired to be king or queen of our own personal hills? Tell the truth, now. Perhaps we want to cling to our view of human nature as naturally good because how else can we rightfully claim such high places?

The parables of the rich man and the laborers in the vineyard exemplify our appetite for personal glory and all that goes with it: status, pecking orders, manipulation—the ability to lord it over others and finally replace God with the self. What we want is radically out of keeping or disordered in terms of the order of God's rule. Would any of us have received the landowner's treatment of the last hired with joy or gladness? Would we have said, "Good for you!" Or would we have stood by and muttered, "Hey, wait a minute!" Further, would we have stopped to question what these merciful actions said about our employer or lender?

No. "We want justice!"

The vineyard owner is just to all, but reserves the right to be gracious. He is gracious even to those who are corrupt enough themselves that they would have him be less so. The parable is a terrible revelation of our self-destructive envy.

Although, as "The Corvair at Midnight" teaches, the image of God within us longs for the love of a good and generous Father. "The Laborers in the Vineyard" parable shows us the human impulse to constrain this love and make it subject to our egos. We want to be accepted wholly and absolutely, but we also want to be accepted more than others. Otherwise, our twisted natures ask, what's the point? As the old saying about writers goes, "It's not enough for you to succeed; your friends must fail." That's a hard truth that applies somewhat to all of us, as the stern rebuke of the landowner to the grumbling workers suggests.

Walker Percy in *Lost In The Cosmos* notes the prevalence of envy and resentment among all classes and intellectual strata. He asks whether a biology professor who learns his colleague has won the Nobel Prize receives this as unadulterated good news, bad news, or a mixture of both?[6] What about the factory worker whose best friend suddenly becomes part of management? Or even the newly engaged woman who finds her friend is planning her wedding a month before her own? The envious self is everywhere.

The scholar René Girard claims that the urge to keep up with the Joneses has played a central role in the formation of culture. Because we want what others want and desire what others desire simply because others do, we find ourselves increasingly frustrated. The tensions of envy and resentment spread from one person to another in a society until entire cultures become volatile. Then societies, according to Girard, find scapegoats to blame and punish for the envious tensions within the collective heart. Girard believes the prevalence of "dying god" myths in almost every primitive culture stems from murderous acts of scapegoating. In other words, since the beginning of time, people have been crucifying others in order to feel good about themselves. In fact, Girard bases an entire theory of cultural formation on this central act of preferring our own good to the good of others.

Our therapeutic society says we have to learn to love ourselves, we have to learn to forgive ourselves. "Learning to love yourself is the greatest love of all!" as first George Benson and then Whitney Houston sang.

Mercy, mercy me. I cannot think of anything more hopeless. That's the last thing we are capable of because it's the first thing we try: it's the problem, not the solution. Our self-love demands storehouses of excess and justice without mercy. Our self-forgiveness cannot deconstruct our envy because then we'd have to give up the standards by which our self-love tries to operate. Our ego is driven by pride like the rich rich young ruler, our appetite is out of control like the rich man, and our emotional lives suffer from a relentless resentment that even corrupts conscience. No wonder we scream out, "I feel so dead inside."

Is God fair? No, he's not, and we should all be thankful of that. If we could demand that God operate by our own sense of fairness, God would have to condemn all of us alike without mercy, for who can claim to have escaped the trap of envy and resentment? "All we like sheep have gone astray," say the Old Testament Scriptures. The New Testament adds: "If we say we are without sin, the truth is not in us." That people are naturally good is simply a lie. Or didn't the reader, like me, feel sympathy with the protest of those first hired?

To me "The Laborers in the Vineyard" parable is one of the most practical parables. Every time I start to whine that things aren't fair, I just remember this parable, and I say, "No one promised fair." Thank goodness.

SECTION III
RECONCILING

CHAPTER EIGHT

HOW GOOD DO WE HAVE TO BE?

OUR REBELLION AGAINST GOD'S LOVE IS NOT SOMETHING WE want to face. For many, the conversation ends here because Jesus holds what we now think of as "absolutist" views. Be perfect, as your Father in heaven is perfect, he says. That's the standard. At the same time he reveals the human person as anything but perfect.

A strange reversal, it would seem, comes about in any conversation with Jesus. We begin addressing our questions to him and end having to question ourselves, to confront the unanswerable dilemma which Jesus poses: the love of God and our deep, if unacknowledged, desire to subvert that love.

So what are we to do?

Not this or that or the other thing. The question, the dilemma, serves only to make tangible an impenetrable barrier. The love of God for humanity, although real and plentiful, cannot embrace us because we cannot open ourselves to it.

The paradox defies every instinct we have. Surely this cannot be right. We will try harder, we will think more positively, we will seek to persuade Jesus otherwise. We keep asking the

question, How good do we have to be? with the thought that
there must be some way to cut a deal. Jesus cannot mean this,
can he?

I remember having a talk with my childhood friend Stuart,
in which as a boy brought up within the Christian faith I
explained that God wants us to be perfect. He asked, Did I want
this? Stuart certainly didn't, and he thought it a bad idea and
even unhealthy. Everyone had to have a few faults or vices in
order to make him interesting, Stuart thought. Else, the person
would miss out on what life was really all about.

And that is . . . pleasure? Getting away with something?
Knowing what others don't?

In part, certainly. We'd like to think our pleasurable vices
harm no one and make life much more bearable for everybody.

Also, we live with the persistent suggestion that a more
profound knowledge of life—both its light and dark sides—
will be to our advantage. Modes of being that we have not experienced hold a strange attraction.

For instance, for some the dangerous person fascinates; they
look to "outsiders" for what they do not find in their own circles.
The good-looking tough guy—James Dean—or the girl from
the wrong side of town—Carole Lombard or Pam Grier—what
wouldn't we give to be like them or have them turn their atten-
tions to us? If we took a hand in saving them from themselves,
they might repay us by vanquishing our boredom.

Some of us regard *ourselves* as orphaned outsiders, and we
are always trying to find a way into the inner circle, to rub shoulders with those in the know. "Oh yeah, I know about that,"
we imply, when giving winking approval to drinking bouts,
sexcapades, or criticisms of the boss. We want to be like insiders, above the common rung.

Whether we look to those outside or those inside, we
cannot escape believing that others can accept and deal with
life in a way we cannot. That they know a secret that will
solve the problem we are to ourselves. If only we had their
hidden knowledge, we could "hot-wire reality," to use song-

writer Jackson Brown's line, and find happiness.

How good do we have to be, Jesus? Are you sure life's about such rigorous virtue? That God's love cannot be content with anything but absolute purity? Perhaps life isn't really about virtue at all, but knowing what escapes others—that we can live on our own terms and get away with it. Like those outsiders, those insiders. Or perhaps someone really knows the answer to the dilemma of God's perfection and our fallibility in a way we can only, very obscurely, anticipate.

THERE'S A RIOT GOING ON

AT 12:14 ON MONDAY, OCTOBER 18, WNBC BROKE INTO local programming with a live report from Harlem, where in the aftermath of a police corruption case, in which three officers were acquitted of assault charges, a riot had broken out.

The helicopter shot from SKY HIGH 4 showed several black youths dragging two Korean shopkeepers from their store. They smashed the store's windows and began looting. When the store owners fought them, the youths' attention turned to the shopkeepers themselves. They pushed the woman down and taunted her.

As the man threw himself toward his wife, he was punched in the face. He slumped to his knees. One youth kicked him in the stomach and the other attacker took his turn as the man sprawled on the ground. The youths lost any interest in the store as they took turns kicking the victims.

SKY HIGH 4 refocused on a nearby building, where a fire had broken out, and then another fire several blocks away.

In the offices of *The National Review*, an editor watched the rioting as he ate lunch and decided to write an editorial about all races—even African-American—being prone to racism. He could work the irony of this to great effect against the liberals.

At *Ms. Magazine*, an editor downed a can of Slim Fast and viewed the same scenes. How much longer would this violence against women go on? The editor recalled her own near rape, and decided she would, after all, write an editorial against Gangsta Rap and its cult of violence. They had crossed the line of mere speech, perpetrating vicarious abuse.

While he enjoyed a falafel, a professor at nearby Auburn Seminary watched the riot and thought of the book he had coming out on Jesus' preference for the poor. The conditions creating such incidents had to be addressed and perhaps his work would initiate a truly constructive dialogue.

Three other people watched these same scenes, realized that they were taking place nearby, and quickly left their homes.

Within a minute or two, at ground zero of the riot, a skinhead arrived.

As did a Hasidic Jew in a Homburg hat and side curls.

And an unemployed middle-aged black man.

The attackers had moved off. The police had not yet arrived. The three suddenly faced each other across the wounded bodies of the Korean couple.

The skinhead asked, "Did anybody call 911?"

"I did," said the Hasid.

"Me, too," said the middle-aged black man.

The Hasid knelt by the woman, as did the black man. She was breathing but unconscious. The skinhead checked out the husband, whose face lay in a pool of his own blood, bits of teeth floating.

The ambulance arrived. Then the police.

"Who called the ambulance?" the detective screamed amid the confusion.

"We did," the three said.

"You'd better get yourselves outta here now," barked a cop.

"I must go with them," said the Hasid, pointing to the ambulance and the techs.

"He's my grocer," said the middle-aged black man. "I'll go."

The skinhead was helping the techs lift the stretcher into the ambulance. Another ambulance arrived and the Korean woman was placed in it.

At the hospital, having each insisted on accompanying the Koreans, the Hasid, the middle-aged black man, and the skinhead waited together in the emergency room. They still did not know what to say to each other. The skinhead and the black man shared a pack of matches to light their cigarettes.

The TV was on. The reporter said, "A report just in. Dave? Dave? There's a report just in that the Korean couple — the victims of a vicious beating, as shown here from SKY HIGH 4 — have been taken to the trauma center at St. Luke's. The man is reported in critical condition."

"Listen, Jorge. Can you hear me, Jorge?"

"Yes, Dave."

"Do we know of any deaths from the rioting to date?"

"No, Dave. The fires broke out in what are believed to be empty buildings. An ambulance worker I spoke with thought the couple would make it, although the man is listed as critical."

"Thanks, Jorge. We're taking it back to the studio now." The anchor turns from profile and looks into the camera. "Harlem seems to be quieting. If any further violence breaks out, WNBC will take you there live."

Getting Inside with the Outsider

AS WE SAID AT THE BEGINNING, JESUS' TEACHING REMAINS a pervasive influence in our culture, enough for most to recognize "There's a Riot Going On" as a variant of the Good Samaritan.

On its surface the Good Samaritan seems to give us every encouragement that we *can* be good enough. Isn't this what made Jesus a good moral teacher, that he encouraged us to be good Samaritans to our neighbors? And doesn't "Riot" further illustrate the possibility of such virtue, even among ethnic or ideological groups—Jews, African-Americans, neo-Nazis—who often view the other as an enemy?

Maybe Jesus' diagnosis of the human condition isn't as dark as previously suggested. Perhaps what we need to know is how we can be good enough to receive God's love.

Jesus actually tells the Good Samaritan parable in response to a question that seeks a negotiated peace with God's perfection and humankind's fallibility. A lawyer approaches Jesus and asks a question to test him: "Master, what must I do to inherit eternal life?"

Jesus tests him right back: "What is your reading of the Law?"

The lawyer knows the conventional answer—the two-sentence summary of the Ten Commandments: "You must love the Lord your God with all your heart, with all your soul, with all your strength, and with all your mind, and your neighbor as yourself."

Jesus tells the man he's answered correctly. "Do this and life is yours."[1]

So far in this exchange there's been little more than sparring with platitudes. The lawyer finds himself unsatisfied, embarrassed. He realizes his subtle, tough question has turned out to be a puffball. The equivalent of asking a constitutional authority to recite the First Amendment. "But the man was anxious to justify himself," the gospel writer Luke tells us. He doesn't want to look a fool, so he poses a contentious follow-up: "And who is my neighbor?"

This was a lively question of the day. The religious authorities preferred a restricted meaning, teaching that one's "neighbor" must be a Jew or a Jewish convert. In other words:

If you do a good turn, know for whom you are doing it,
And your good deeds will not go to waste.
Do good to a devout man. . . .
Do not go to the help of a sinner,
Do good to a humble man,
Give nothing to a godless one,
Refuse him bread, do not give him any,
For the Most High himself detests sinners.[2]

For Jews no Samaritan could ever be classified as anything but a sinner. The adjective "good" has for so long been
attached to "Samaritan" that we fail, right off, to experience
the description as an oxymoron, a contradiction like "the
unjust judge." But Jesus' audience would have been horrified
at the notion that a Samaritan could ever be called "good."

The Samaritans were despised by the Jews for establishing
a rival offshoot of Judaism—a heretical sect. The Samaritans
despised their despisers. A centuries-long running feud resulted,
with provocative acts on both sides. The Samaritans protested
the rebuilding of Jerusalem's walls after the Babylonian exile,
making a precarious political situation much worse. In turn,
John Hyrcanius, Jewish governor and priest, marched on the
Samaritan sanctuary at Shechem in 128 B.C. and destroyed it.

Not long before Jesus told this parable, the Samaritans, as
Josephus records in his *Antiquities*, had thrown a heap of
human bones into the temple courtyard during Passover, thus
defiling the ritual purity of that holy place. Because contact
with a human corpse incurred the highest degree of ritual
impurity, the Samaritans effectively stopped the celebration,
underlining their view of it as invalid. The memory of this incident was still fresh in the minds of Jesus' audience.

To hear the parable as Jesus' audience, we have to conjure
up a hero we hate for what we believe to be good and sufficient reasons. Neo-Nazis do it for many Jews (and me as well).
Jews do it for some blacks. Blacks and Jews do it for neo-
Nazis—thus my three Samaritans in "There's a Riot Going On."

Not only do we misunderstand the parable of the Good Samaritan because we lack a visceral reaction to it, but the parable itself has been so influential in Western culture that we are too quick to judge the failings of the priest and perhaps even the Levite. The description of the man attacked by robbers is crucial in this respect.

> "A man was going down from Jerusalem to Jericho, and fell into the hands of robbers, who stripped him, beat him, and went away, leaving him half dead. Now by chance a priest was going down that road; and when he saw him, he passed by on the other side. So likewise a Levite, when he came to the place and saw him, passed by on the other side. But a Samaritan while traveling came near him; and when he saw him, he was moved with pity. He went to him and bandaged his wounds, having poured oil and wine on them. Then he put him on his own animal, brought him to an inn, and took care of him. The next day he took out two denarii, gave them to the innkeeper, and said, 'Take care of him; and when I come back, I will repay you whatever more you spend.' Which of these three, do you think, was a neighbor to the man who fell into the hands of the robbers?"[3]

The man is stripped and half-dead—presumably unconscious. Given these circumstances, the priest actually does what his religion tells him to do. He should help a devout man (a Jew) and shun a godless one. In this instance, how is the priest to know whether the victim is a Jew or not? The priest has neither the man's language nor his clothing by which to identify him as a Jew. So he cannot be sure about the ethical nature of rendering aid.

The priest also knows that if he discovers that the man is dead, he will incur ritual impurity. In fact, he cannot get any closer than four cubits—about seven feet—to a corpse. If the priest incurs ritual impurity, he cannot collect, distribute, and feed himself and his household from the tithes of the people — nor perform the services he's likely to have promised on his arrival in Jericho. Ritual impurity would prohibit him from carrying out his religious vocation, at least until he had undergone a week-long period of ritual purification and sacrificed a red heifer.

The priest's obligations of charity are conditional, but those of ritual impurity are unconditional, so he does the prudent thing and passes by.

The Levite, a member of the tribe chosen to assist the Jews' priests, presents a more ambiguous case. Even if he touches a corpse and incurs ritual impurity, the ritual purification he must undergo will be much less arduous. And he can continue his nonreligious activities without interruption. The Levite may be able to see the priest before him on the road, though, as he seems to take his cues from the priest's interpretation of the Law. Also, the road from Jerusalem down to Jericho was notoriously dangerous and the Levite would naturally be concerned for his own safety. If he pauses too long, he may be attacked himself. Whatever his motives, the Levite does not act.

The Samaritan comes upon this scene with a different set of worries, but ones that are no less pressing; indeed, they may be even more severe. He faces our common apprehension that no good act goes unpunished for specific reasons. His own sect has laws of ritual impurity, which have their own stringent consequences. Then, if the victim turns out to be a Jew, the Samaritan may receive nothing but scorn. Even the oil and wine that the Samaritan uses to bind up the man's wounds were not to be accepted by Jews from Samaritans. The Samaritan would naturally worry for his own safety as well.

Moreover, Samaritans were so hated by the Jews that any relatives arriving to care for the victim might well assume that the Samaritan himself is responsible for the victim's injuries. At the time, Middle Eastern notions of justice, including those of the Jews, allowed for homicidal reprisals. What would a Jewish family have presumed if they found an injured family member in the company of a Samaritan? That the Samaritan had committed the crime. Explaining the situation, the scholar Kenneth Bailey asks what westerners would have presumed if a Native American had brought an injured cowboy into town and then stayed with him overnight at the local hotel.[4] A Sioux brave might well have been strung up before the circumstances of the cowboy's injury could be made clear.

The Samaritan then not only puts himself out, he puts himself in a good deal of danger. Yet, knowing the shady character of most innkeepers in that day, he promises to return, in order to insure that his money is well spent and that the bill is paid in full.

Considered in this light, this parable—so well-known to many of us—becomes again a shocking story. We are asked to be charitable at all times to the point of putting our lives in grave danger even for people we hate on principle.

How are we to do this? Through the parable of the Good Samaritan, Jesus not only addresses the background discussion to the lawyer's question, "Who is my neighbor?" but he also suggests how strange the fulfillment of his command to perfection might appear.

Many commentators have noted that after the priest and Levite, the audience might have expected a common Jew to happen along the road, in which case the story would simply hook the lawyer's fancy self-justifications with an egalitarian barb. Instead, Jesus chooses a figure, the Samaritan, whom no one in the crowd could be expected to find sympathetic— a figure who probably made everyone fighting mad. Again, just imagine standing in downtown Tel Aviv today and telling a story featuring a "Good Palestinian," in which a Palestinian aids a victimized Jew. Who would want to tell such a story and why?

Remember that this conversation began with a man saying he lived by the Law and wanted eternal life. In commenting on the Law and his own mission, Jesus says, "Do not think that I have come to abolish the law or the prophets; I have come not to abolish but to fulfill."[5]

The Samaritan likewise fulfills the Law when he loves his neighbor as himself. It makes me wonder whether Jesus sees himself as the Good Samaritan. I don't mean literally. We know from his talk with the woman at the well[6] that Jesus disagreed with Samaritan thinking. Jesus says to this woman, "You Samaritans worship what you do not know; we worship what we do know, for salvation is from the Jews." So why would he tell a story in which a Samaritan fulfills the Law—with a heroic virtue far surpassing what any of us might want to attempt? Was Jesus preparing us to see *him* as the answer to our dilemma? This is the true genius and mystery of the parable, I think.

By choosing the Samaritan as the parable's hero, Jesus comments extensively on his own mission. Only someone acting contrary to all conventional expectations can truly be the expression of God's love—someone like Jesus himself.

The Good Samaritan parable also makes use of what I feel must be a universal suspicion—that someone knows something we don't. This obscure and yet prevalent notion, which drives us both outward from the comfort of our own inner circles and inward toward a secret knowledge, prepares us to accept that there might be a Good Samaritan—someone close by and yet unknown—who knows what we do not know and therefore can do for us what we cannot do for ourselves. This suspicion prepares us for the idea of a savior. A savior knows what we need to know and does what we cannot do.

At the same time, a savior transcends both the attractive outsider and the seductive insider; a savior is better than a James Dean or any inner circle because in either case we are always left looking on, unsatisfied. (Groucho Marx once sent the following note to an exclusive club: "Please accept my resignation. I don't want to belong to any club that will accept me as a member."[7]) A savior takes us out of ourselves and into his company. His mission in fact destroys all distinctions of insider versus outsider and, in doing so, establishes the unity among peoples and between God and humankind that the apostle Paul later speaks of in his letter to the Galatians:

The law was like those Greek tutors, with which you are familiar, who escort children to school and protect them from danger or distraction, making sure the children will really get to the place they set out for.

But now you are in direct relationship with God. Your baptism in Christ was not just washing you up for a fresh start. It also involved dressing you in an adult faith wardrobe—Christ's life, the fulfillment of God's original promise.

In Christ's family there can be no division into Jew and non-Jew, slave and free, male and female. Among us you are all equal. That is, we are all in a common relationship with Jesus Christ. Also, since you are Christ's family, then you are Abraham's famous "descendant," heirs according to the covenant promises.[8]

As Paul makes clear, we cannot fulfill the Law ourselves—we cannot be good enough or know enough. The Law reveals utter perfection. It leads us to see our utter inadequacy; that all our righteousness, all our good intentions, our good deeds, our spiritual ambitions, even our "correct thinking"—be it the correctness of the *National Review*, *Ms. Magazine*, or the seminary—becomes disgusting in comparison with the standard. So Jesus must not only be "good teacher" but "good Samaritan" as well. Jesus will suffer the full consequences of the Samaritan's risks—a murderous retaliation against innocence. He will give his life as a ransom—the full payment to the innkeeper—so that we may be healed. He is the one who, once again, comes along and finds us in our helplessness and cares for us. He dresses our wounds, provides for our healing and comfort, and makes sure that his own efforts are not squandered but prevail in an evil world. Most of all, a savior forgives us. He sees how we neglect our neighbors and makes up for our limited notions of virtue and the ways we use them to betray the real thing.

The question becomes, When we wake up and see Jesus as our Good Samaritan, what do we say? Are we grateful?

CHAPTER NINE

IS GRACE TRULY AMAZING?

IN THE LAST CHAPTER WE SAW THAT JESUS POSITIONS *HIMSELF* as the answer to the dilemma of God's perfection and humankind's failings. We cannot be good enough for God, and so God in the Son condescends to be our Good Samaritan. Once again we are asked to accept ourselves as needing help— specifically forgiveness for our hostility toward God.

The notion of a savior who forgives and heals us, like the notion of God's merciful love, can be an outrage. In one of his letters, Peter calls it "a stone of stumbling and a rock of offense."[1]

I remember having a memorable talk with an older writer. His judgment of a thinly disguised autobiographical character (me) struck me as harsh. I pointed out that in the short story we were considering, my character later apologizes for not being able to respond compassionately to an older woman's romantic entreaty.

"What do we think of people who apologize, Harold?" he asked.

I didn't know how to respond at the time, but I've thought

about what he was saying long and hard since.

"Never complain, never explain" encapsulates the view this mentor hoped I would arrive at. Those who don't have the character to make their choices and suffer whatever consequences ensue aren't worthy of respect. We detest those who apologize, and for good reason: because they are asking to be excused from reality and have us collude in their escapism.

Those who embrace "never complain, never explain" take life straight up. If they were to awake in the presence of a strange rescuer, whoever might be a Samaritan to them, they would recognize their own innocence, the violent and sometimes chaotic nature of the world ("these things happen"), and be appropriately grateful to their unlikely benefactor. Then they would pick themselves up and get on with their lives without another thought.

Isn't this the state of emotional maturity and character formation to which we should all aspire? Isn't this what knowing oneself is all about? Why should such a simple story like "The Good Samaritan" be made out to have a depth and volume that engulfs us all? Some of us simply see no need of a god who can do for us what we can't do for ourselves. In fact, the idea strikes us as the sick wish-fulfillment fantasy of life's cowards. If we can take it, so can they, and frankly, they'd be better off if they did.

Is forgiveness a good idea then? Is grace truly amazing? Even if we cannot satisfy Jesus' demand for perfection, isn't the world a better place when we all make our choices and suffer the consequences? Doesn't the whole idea of a forgiving God just encourage people to act badly? Doesn't Jesus see that he's encouraging the very behavior he's against?

UNDER EVERY GREEN TREE

In 1955 A YOUNG WOMAN MET HER FUTURE HUSBAND AT THE University of Arizona. She dropped out of college to marry and went to work as a secretary, putting her husband through law school.

Once her husband found a job in a Tempe firm, they started a family and had two girls before a third child, a son, was stillborn. The girls called their daddy "Yum-yums" because he made up for working overtime with the candies he found, magically, behind the girls' ears.

The husband made partner, which did not decrease the time he spent working; the demands on his time only grew. When not working, he ran with his old fraternity brothers, played golf and tennis, and went to sports bars to watch Monday Night Football.

Tempted to resent this, his wife reasoned that with the rigors of his practice he needed to blow off steam. He provided well for her and the girls, and if their sex life had become dull to the point of indifference, she had never been that interested anyway.

Then, alarmingly, her husband was arrested in a sweep of the southside hotels by the vice department. The prostitute he solicited turned out to be a cop.

There were apologies, many apologies.

His suspension from the Bar did not last long, it turned out, and chastened, he promised to keep his nose to the grindstone.

Three years went by and all seemed fine, except the grindstone turned for fourteen to fifteen hours every day.

He was making a considerable amount of money, and they decided to move into another house, even though the girls would soon be in college. They wanted a place where the anticipated grandkids could visit, as well as a few niceties for themselves: a quiet setting on a larger lot, a private tennis court, even a spa like the one their friends the Parkers had just installed.

As the woman cleaned out the basement prior to inviting a realtor in, she came upon a cardboard file box in the storage area behind the stairs where her husband kept his sports equipment. She wondered whether to toss it, then looked inside. There she found individual files crammed with Polaroids taken with their Swinger camera. These showed her husband and almost every wife in the neighborhood in what are known as "compromising positions."

When she confronted her husband, he protested that the photos were old and that many of the women had moved out of the neighborhood.

She left him.

This meant setting up in a two-bedroom apartment, not far from the southside hotel where her husband had once been arrested. She had no money of her own and no idea where to find a job.

Everyone advised her to divorce, but she had thoughts of her own on this matter and refused—even when her husband pressed her to do the same. (This was in the days before "no-fault" divorce, when the more offended might resist.) Her husband was willing to give her alimony. It turned out that he wanted to marry his nineteen-year-old girlfriend.

She took a job, almost the same job she had twenty years earlier, working as a secretary, this time at the university. At night, she finished her degree in the new continuing education program. With the aid of additional student loans, she went on to attend law school herself.

As a result of these circumstances, her girls had to work their way through college. Their father withheld his financial support in order to pressure their mother. "Tell her this is ridiculous," the father said. "Tell her to give me the divorce and everyone can be happy."

When this did not avail, the death threats started. Unknown

women and men called the woman with terse messages like, "Take out some life insurance, your girls are going to need the money" and "I'm talking to a dead person." She found the handle of her front door smashed to bits one night and received videotapes in the mail of her girls being surreptitiously observed going about their daily activities. The audio included horrible muttering threats.

The woman took no action; she waited.

When she graduated from law school and passed the Bar, she filed suit against her husband for defamation of character. She had kept the box of pictures, and now presented these before the court, arguing that her husband had traduced her inalienable dignity in the eyes of everyone they knew and thus had committed a de facto form of libel.

The woman could not win the suit in court, as she knew, but her skills in bringing the matter to trial won her a job with the best firm in Arizona. The court of public opinion voted almost unanimously for her as well. The judge offered to expedite any divorce proceeding she might bring, but this was not what she wanted.

The negative publicity effectively ended her husband's career — even without anyone ever hearing of his death-threat harassment campaign. He lost his job, and no one would hire him when he started chasing ambulances.

In despair, he started to drink heavily.

Then the woman suddenly reversed field and told her husband (for they were still married) that if he would clean himself up, he could move into the home she had recently purchased. She had enough of this world's goods for them both now.

Her husband couldn't believe the offer. He suspected she was out to drive him crazy. He even feared violence on her part.

The woman implored him. She told him she couldn't be more serious. She had never set out to destroy him, only bring him to his senses. That had taken the most extreme of reality therapies. But it was over with now. He should come home.

Her husband simply ran, taking what he considered revenge by mailing back new Polaroids of himself and various women.

She could see from the pictures that he was rail-thin and looked tubercular. The women became older and more sallow-skinned and the labels on the whiskey bottles cheaper.

In time coworkers, judges, and even clients asked the newly famous attorney out. She told them thank you, she was married. This was not easy. Her voluntary chastity brought with it a racing sexual desire she had never known before. Still, she lived quietly, in hope.

Five years later her husband appeared at her door. At first she thought him a vagrant, asking for a handout. But when she saw his blue eyes, still fired by an icy Northern light despite the broken blood vessels, she asked him straight in.

"No, no," he said. "I don't want to bother you." He was standing in the fierce Southwest sunshine in an old suit that looked boiled.

Finally, he came out with it. "Can you lend me five hundred dollars, Gayle?" he asked. "I know I don't deserve it, but I need it."

He looked around him as if he were being hunted.

She went inside the house and came back with a check, waving it so the ink would dry. She had written it out to him and signed it, but left the amount blank.

He took a brief, astonished look. "Why would you do this?" he asked.

"We're still married, Adam. Everything I have is yours." She reached for his hand. "I wish you'd come in."

He took her hand and stepped across the threshold into her embrace. She kissed his weathered face, his neck.

The girls were horrified at their parents' reconciliation, particularly when their mother insisted that their father should be asked to give the eldest away at her upcoming wedding.

"He threatened to kill you! He had us videotaped. He's a creep!" the eldest shrieked.

"You used to call him 'Yum-Yums,' don't you remember?" their mother asked.

"Mom, he gave us penny candies so he could go whoring," the younger said. "He practically disowned us."

"I don't want him meeting Phil's family," the eldest said. "I don't want them ever to know anything about him. I told Phil he was dead. He is dead—to me. I want him to stay that way."

"He was dead," their mother agreed. "But now you have the choice of letting him live again. Will you? Please, girls?"

Proving It

NO MATTER HOW OFTEN WE SEE IT, THERE'S ALWAYS SOMETHING strange and unexpected about people turning against one another and becoming enemies. How does it happen? Someone takes an immediate dislike to us—or we to them. Or, through a series of bewildering circumstances, we find ourselves in the situation of having to fire someone from a job—or getting fired ourselves. There's a sister or a brother that we rarely see, for reasons neither of us likes to talk about—or even understands much. A romance looks like the perfect relationship and ends how things always end, badly, but this time even worse, with a nasty spike.

If we've lived for any length of time, someone leaps to mind during these reflections. Someone we hate, legitimately, justifiably. It's strange but true, we really have enemies. We may not be the other's enemy, but we are not going to let them get away with anything, either. Not anymore.

Never complain, never explain, and *never again.* The third "never" seems to be an unavoidable extension in this world.

Jesus tells a story that we usually think of in connection with a character as lost as anyone could be—the prototypical lost child.

119

But the story can also be seen as the context for a long build-up to a final confrontation with a "never complain, never explain" type. In fact, this second figure in Jesus' story, like the daughters from "Under Every Green Tree," finds his identity in his hard-working, dependable nature. Let's take a different look at one of Jesus' best-known stories, "The Prodigal Son."

> Then Jesus said, "There was a man who had two sons. The younger of them said to his father, 'Father, give me the share of the property that will belong to me.' So he divided his property between them. A few days later the younger son gathered all he had and traveled to a distant country, and there he squandered his property in dissolute living. When he had spent everything, a severe famine took place throughout that country, and he began to be in need. So he went and hired himself out to one of the citizens of that country, who sent him to his fields to feed the pigs. He would gladly have filled himself with the pods that the pigs were eating; and no one gave him anything. But when he came to himself he said, 'How many of my father's hired hands have bread enough and to spare, but here I am dying of hunger! I will get up and go to my father, and I will say to him, "Father, I have sinned against heaven and before you; I am no longer worthy to be called your son; treat me like one of your hired hands."' So he set off and went to his father. But while he was still far off, his father saw him and was filled with compassion; he ran and put his arms around him and kissed him. Then the son said to him, 'Father, I have sinned against heaven and before you; I am no longer worthy to be called your son.' But the father said to his slaves, 'Quickly, bring out a robe—the best one—and put it on him; put a ring on his finger and sandals on his feet. And get the fatted calf and kill it, and let us eat and celebrate; for this son of mine was dead and is

Is Grace Truly Amazing?

alive again; he was lost and is found!' And they began
to celebrate. Now his elder son was in the field; and
when he came and approached the house, he heard
music and dancing. He called one of the slaves and
asked what was going on. He replied, 'Your brother has
come, and your father has killed the fatted calf,
because he has got him back safe and sound.' Then he
became angry and refused to go in. His father came
out and began to plead with him. But he answered his
father, 'Listen! For all these years I have been working
like a slave for you, and I have never disobeyed your
command; yet you have never given me even a young
goat so that I might celebrate with my friends. But
when this son of yours came back, who has devoured
your property with prostitutes, you killed the fatted
calf for him!' Then the father said to him, 'Son, you are
always with me, and all that is mine is yours. But we
had to celebrate and rejoice, because this brother of
yours was dead and has come to life; he was lost and
has been found.'"[2]

The story of the prodigal son is one of three that Jesus tells in
the gospel of Luke in response to the Pharisee's protests against
his eating with sinners. From the beginning of the story, the
wisdom of forgiving others—to the point of being willing to
appear as their friend—is in play. That Jesus ate with "pub-
licans and sinners" caused the religious authorities no end of
consternation; to them it denied the very basis of the Jewish
faith: that one must separate oneself from evil in order to
cleave to God. God might be a forgiving God, but the Most
High didn't forgive just anybody. God's forgiveness had to be
earned through keeping God's Law. Those who made no
attempt to do so simply had to be avoided for the sake of one's
own purity. When Jesus ate with sinners, he made it seem as
if God didn't care about obedience. In their own way, the
Pharisees embraced a "never complain, never explain" doctrine.

The benefit of God's blessing went to those who deserved it and no others. They didn't want to hear about apologies.

It's hard for us to imagine the scandal Jesus caused by eating with sinners, except to imagine an entire culture devoted to "never complain, never explain." Likewise, it's hard for us to grasp the scandalous nature of "The Prodigal Son." Its depths of evil are much greater than we may at first imagine.

Rebellious teenagers have become such stock characters, even glamorized ones, that the younger son's actions may strike us as a typical, if regrettable, rite of passage. But every element in the story must have shocked Jesus' audience.

First, within the entire body of Middle Eastern literature, both ancient and modern, no son ever asks for his inheritance before the death of his father. The word translated *property* in Jesus' story might be better rendered as "living," for in Greek the word is *bios*, which means "life" or "living." The father divides his life between his two sons. The transliteration more adequately conveys the identification of the father with his lands. He is utterly dependent on the produce of these lands and his sons' roles as managers and workers. This was the only form of social security known in New Testament Israel.

Patriarchs were generally counseled by wisdom literature not to make bequests until breathing their last. Early assignment of an inheritance occurred, usually in cases, it seems, in which the father wished to restrict his inheritance to the sons of one marriage rather than another. The father still expected to be supported by the produce of the land, however. That was the usual pattern and perhaps the exclusive one.

The younger son, who is assigned and disposes of what can be assumed to be a third (his rightful portion as a younger sibling) of the family's land, expresses by his behavior, to the Middle Eastern mind, nothing less than a death wish toward his father. He is taking from him his living, his *bios*.

Yet, his father grants his request. Here the naturalism of the story is crossed with such an unexpected or "magic" element that we should hear distant trumpets of God's arrival.

Jesus' audience would have wanted the story to back up at this point, to ask pointed questions of the elder brother. It would have been his role to forestall any such request to the father; a patriarch should never have heard of such a thing. Yet, the elder son allows for the early assignment of two-thirds of the property to himself. He benefits and says nothing. His lack of action would have been seen as complicity in the younger son's virtual crime — as aiding and abetting.

Further, the elder brother's passivity suggests that he, too, is in some measure estranged from his father. Without these suspicions in our own minds we may see the father's final dialogue with the elder as an epilogue, almost a tacked-on moral. "The Prodigal Son," though, is really a double or even triple tale, in which the conclusion makes a point that keeps expanding.

When the younger brother finds himself in a pigsty mess — a squeamish nightmare for a Jew — he plans out his apology and chooses a course of action designed to smooth things over with his angry father. He will become a hired hand. Not a slave, it's important to note, for as a slave he would become once again part of his family's household. He still wants to maintain a measure of independence; as a hired hand, he may live in the town; perhaps, he may be able to make a measure of restitution through repayment. What the younger brother imagines falls explicitly within the confines of a legal transaction. He does not expect forgiveness. He wants to negotiate a new deal — a sweetheart deal, it's true, given what he's done, but a deal nevertheless.

The instant the father starts running toward the son, Jesus' audience would have gasped. Middle Eastern patriarchs do not run, ever. They are known by the dignity of their slow-measured walk, as a soldier is known by his smart step or a bridal procession by its stately progress. But the father runs to meet the younger brother. This may not be motivated simply by pure joy. The younger brother has broken such a serious taboo that the villagers may greet him with taunts and denunciations, and perhaps beat him up. The father may be running to stave this off. He greets his son as quickly as possible to let his neighbors know how he would have his son received; he forsakes his pride to ensure the whole community's welcome.

The father lets his young son get through no more than the prepared confession of repentance before he makes an unexpected offer: absolute forgiveness and restoration.

The story does not comment on this directly, but the younger son has to accept this grace, leaving behind his legal thinking—his plans for a negotiated surrender—to enter into the joy of being a true son. This he does. But how easily? Which is to say, I can't help wondering whether he doesn't pause for a moment as he realizes that he must give up any pretense to independence. The momentum of someone's estrangement can often carry him along in destructive behavior. Mercy is sometimes hard to receive; its acceptance means we have been really and truly wrong. In this case, the younger brother's confession is not merely a form of bargaining, but genuine. He is prepared to be restored. He forgets about asking to be a hired hand, and dispenses with his thoughts of a deal.

His father kisses him. He declares the son's passage from death to life.

The celebration commences.

The elder brother comes in from the fields and, hearing the music, keeps himself apart. This action verifies his estrangement from his father. The older son in a Middle Eastern household often appeared barefoot to entering guests to indicate that, for the sake of his father's hospitality, he was putting himself in the position of his father's servant. The eldest served as the functional host, the master of ceremonies, who saw to it that his father's guests were cared for. By keeping himself apart, the elder brother silently asks for the father to come out to him, which would have been a humiliation and disgrace to the father.

Once again, the father condescends to his child; he forsakes his own dignity and honor by going out to the elder brother.

In the following dialog, the elder brother's reasoning subtly follows the same lines as the younger's rebellion. His father has never even given him a goat so that he could celebrate with his friends. He wants perquisites, too. He wants his own domestic version of the younger's high old time. He sees his relationship with his father in a master-servant context—he has worked "like a slave." So he wants contractual equity.

The father points out that they are not talking about a labor dispute but life and death, as it springs from bonds of love.

The father invites both of his sons into another world entirely; one in which relationships are based not on contractual rights but on personal and absolute commitment, in which we are united with one another to the extent of knowing as we are known.

The ultimate realization of this awaits heaven, but Jesus identifies our family relationships as signs of the union into which he wishes to draw us. The motions of the heart that tell us love never dies, the impulse to love the beloved beyond any possible circumstance—these are real in God's world.

We do not hear the older brother's response. The tale doubles, but without absolute closure, I think, in order to triple and then multiply without end. For the greatest genius in this parable is found in its incompleteness.

We are forced to complete the story by agreeing with the father's actions or the elder son's reasoning. Again, a reversal comes into play: We read the story only to find it reading our hearts. What do we believe in? A world in which love is the final word or one that's all about getting our rightful share?

The wife, mother, and star attorney, Gayle, in "Under Every Green Tree" exemplifies the same unstinting, patient, everlasting, and unearthly love as the father in "The Prodigal Son." A supernatural love, I can't help but say, that both insists on doing what's right and never stops inviting back into relationship the person whose actions have betrayed that love.

The father's elder son and Gayle's daughters want to maintain, at least initially, that life should be all about making one's choices and suffering the consequences without complaint—

or at least, if there are complaints, they are directed only toward those who disturb or violate this order. They've adopted a "never complain, never explain" attitude and its inevitably attendant "never again."

Jesus tells us through "The Prodigal Son" that because of his Father's love and God's willingness to extend mercy—even to those who have harbored death wishes against him—the world can participate in God's kingdom where forgiveness and reconciliation are the final realities. But these realities come into operation only for those—like the younger brother and Gayle's husband, Peter—who regret their betrayals and accept mercy when it's offered. If the elder brother finally turns away from the celebration, he will cut himself off from his father's love as effectively as his wastrel brother once did. If the two daughters cannot rejoice in their father's return to the life of their family, they will suffer the death of broken relationships that their father once preferred.

The person of great natural common sense and industry often resists, in his or her own way, openness to the love of God as effectively as any scoundrel. The love of God is a scandal. It makes the world a place where everything good about life doesn't have to be earned and the consequences of bad behavior can be forgiven. It seems to deny the principles of good order that make the practical person who he or she is. God's love becomes offensive.

The "never complain, never explain" person may want to interject at this point: Well, these are nice stories, but I don't see anyone loving others like that. For every father who gives his son a break, there are more who run off with other women and never pay child support. For every woman who remains faithful to her husband through bad times, there are more who opt out. In fact, shouldn't people opt out when they've been betrayed? Isn't this the meaning of contemporary freedom as we know it? "The Prodigal Son" isn't a description of the real world and shouldn't be.

The realities spoken of in "The Prodigal Son" certainly need to be verified. We need to know God loves us absolutely no matter what we do. We need to know God forgives us when we regret our betrayals of his love. We need a reason to believe that God gives us the ability to follow Jesus' instructions to "love our enemies" and to pray "forgive us our evils, just as we forgive those who do evil against us." The sting that comes with any thought of an enemy warns us this will not be easy, if it's even possible.

Jesus tells his followers that it's necessary that he die—that he be killed for what he's saying and doing, for who he is.[3] Why is this?

In "The Good Samaritan" the person who extends aid does not experience the undeserved violence that he has every reason to fear. In "The Prodigal Son," the father does not die, despite the patricidal impulses of his two children. These threats do not mature. But the threat of what Jesus is saying to the established order, to a merciless world of getting one's own, does provoke that order to insist that mercy be denied. Jesus, who has committed no wrong other than proclaiming mercy, is killed. He tells his followers at his arrest that he could summon twelve legions of angels—72,000. But he will let his legal assassination take place, nonetheless. He's either deluded in this, or he is, as one of those crucified with him recognizes, an innocent victim. He chooses to let himself be sacrificed that we may believe in a love that prefers its own death to ours. For without someone to verify that such sacrifice is possible and indeed expresses the nature of God's love, we would never believe it. Jesus' passion, his willing death, verifies that "The Prodigal Son" is not just a nice story; it's how God works.

CHAPTER TEN

HOW SHOULD WE
RESPOND TO JESUS?

WE HAVE ARRIVED AT A PRECINCT OF RELIGIOUS EXPERIENCE
that most contemporary people consider out of bounds—that
shadowed valley of death. Our choices seem to have narrowed
to considering ourselves prodigals or envious elder brothers.
Or an Arizona husband and wife who love in a way that doesn't
respect psychotherapeutic boundaries and appears self-
destructive. The father in the prodigal son parable may have
once appeared the great, longed-for fulfillment of the child
within us, but to adopt this posture for ourselves—especially
when read through the wife in "Under Every Green Tree"—
leaves us either actively opposed or frustrated by its impossibility. Let these last figures be images of God then, for they
aren't us, and maybe not even the God we want.

What's affirming about this? It seems more like a guilt trip.
We are being informed of our inevitable failings. And by Jesus.
The attractive storyteller, the ironic opponent of conventional
authority, the poet of divine and all-embracing love has somehow become our accuser. We may have previously made a
space for Jesus outside of institutional religion; we don't want

to consider him an adversary or think of ourselves as hostile toward him. But even considered through his storytelling, Jesus' own teachings turn out to ask us questions for which we have no good answers. He's tricked us somehow into seeing our faults and something even beyond our faults: the human condition as disaster. We both long for God and actively prevent ourselves from finding God. We must rely on Jesus to do for us what we cannot do for ourselves.

The conversation ends right here for many because our own view of Jesus must change or be abandoned or simply forgotten. We want to see Jesus as a wise man who encourages our better angels. Who calls us to fulfill our potential. Who presents an ethic that makes sense—without its supernatural window dressing. The kind of sense that will bring peace and unity to the world whenever the human race makes enough progress to embrace it.

But instead we are asked to respond positively to something entirely negative. To see ourselves as people who hate the way God works and the way God loves. And not just casually or intermittently. Jesus seems to be saying that the source of humanity's and our own problems comes out of this essential antipathy toward God.

We cannot do anything about it, either. We have to rely on the Good Samaritan to do for us what we cannot do for ourselves. We have to place ourselves in Jesus' hands to make a phenomenal transition, like the prodigal and perhaps his elder brother, from death to life.

Let's say we are willing to do this. Doesn't there yet remain a question as to how? Surely something must be required if only to communicate, on our part, that we've come to agree with Jesus' views and are willing to let him be our Good Samaritan.

What do you want from us, Jesus? How do we let you accomplish in our lives what we cannot?

THE VET AND THE LOBBYIST

THE LOBBYIST HAD JUST WITNESSED A VOTE THAT REPRESENTED the biggest victory of his career. His corporate client's new fighter jet might never see action, but Congress nonetheless wanted to see twenty-five of them built, which would earn him a two-million-dollar bonus. His windfall blew away all his common concerns and carried him down the Capital steps and across the Mall. He suddenly felt like taking a walk, despite his bad leg.

Before the doctor gave him the diagnosis, he thought gout was a literary disease, like apoplexy. Too many buttery croissants, finely marbled steaks, and Beauvais wines — the heavy reds with big noses and oak-fine draws he liked. Too many cigars as well, of course, like the Cuban he had in his teeth now but hadn't lit as a measure of discipline. His gouty right leg already minced his fat man's pinch-kneed gait — he didn't want it to get any worse.

Somehow he didn't feel right, and it wasn't the leg. Given the fine spring day, the cherry trees in full white blossom, and the young women showing their legs, he should have been tripping along in his own fat-boy ecstasy, but an uncommon preoccupation kept making itself felt, like someone looking over his shoulder.

A voice told him that the victory had come too easily. Not that he hadn't worked for it. He had made calls, sent faxes, visited every office open to him, counted heads, and astutely refined his lines of argument as he saw how each played. He even hand-delivered a fighter-pilot helmet to the head of the appropriations subcommittee. In the end the funding came through only because of shrewd horse-trading he'd engineered.

Two million made sense for a multibillion-dollar contract that had looked dead in the water early in the year. What was bugging him? Maybe only that he didn't have to worry about anything. Not money at least. Not anymore.

The lobbyist stopped to catch his breath at the top of a small rise. Below him lay the Vietnam War Memorial and an expanding circle of camouflage and khaki-clad veterans. A blare of speech-making filled the air. A man in a wheelchair addressed the crowd from a temporary platform. The old peace symbol around his neck bumped his hand-held microphone as he spoke.

Leading up to Memorial Day, the various veterans groups must be taking turns at remembering history. Today, the group's banner declared, the last stalwarts of Vietnam Veterans Against the War had turned out.

"So now Robert McNamara's come clean, hasn't he?" the man in the wheelchair asked, an electric fire to his voice.

A derisive cheer went up.

"It was all a 'tragic mistake,'" the vet speaker said. "A 'tragic mistake.' What a load!"

The crowd's jeers became angrier.

"Have I been in this chair for thirty years because of a 'tragic mistake'? Did my buddies die because of a 'tragic mistake'? No! No! What our government did was wrong! It was a crime against you and me and this whole country, as well as Vietnam!"

The crowd broke out in a collective shout of such grief and anger that a subterranean thunder seemed to roll back under the lobbyist's feet. At first the lobbyist could only think, "What does the gimp know?" but then, as if in reply, his uneasiness increased. It was almost as if he had forgotten himself, spoken aloud, and been overheard by the vets.

"What will they give us now that we've been proven right?" asked the speaker. "Well, I'll tell you, I don't want anyone giving me anything. I'm taking what's rightfully mine. The right to consider myself a true patriot. The right to remember what really happened. The right to tell future generations the truth! And the capital 'T' truth is this: That we were right and they were wrong!"

"News flash, film at eleven," the lobbyist thought. But just as he prepared to dismiss the episode, he felt as if someone must be eyeing his fashionable if tent-like two-thousand-dollar suit. He looked around him, glaring. "Okay, so here I am," he thought, "Mr. Fat Cat—the military industrial complex's halftime show. What of it?"

But no one was looking at him.

"We did what we could to stop the war machine," the speaker went on. "We are still trying to stop the lying machine. America still doesn't know what to think—what side to be on. At least there's an appreciation for the vets who sacrificed themselves. That's fine, that's good, but it's not enough. Those responsible have to say they were wrong. They have to say it! They have to say it to us!"

The crowd started to chant: "Say it! Say it! Say it! Say it!"

What would the lobbyist say? He actually felt compelled to answer these freaks. The gimp was making him that angry. "If it had been up to me," the lobbyist's thoughts began, "that Wall would have stretched around Washington."

"Say it! Say it! Say it!"

The thunder of the crowd's chant kept pumping volume into his unexpected admission. Around Washington? Did he mean that?

"Say it! Say it! Say it! Say it!"

The names of some of his own buddies were on that wall. He couldn't have meant . . . The mascot costume became leaden. He was coming to feel more the man in the iron mask; his life-time of lying for a living having trapped him.

The speaker punched the air with his microphone-gripping fist in time with the crowd's chants. "Say it! Say it!"

For the first time as an adult the lobbyist found himself almost praying. "Good God."

The speaking vet rolled to the side of the platform where a phalanx of his buddies prepared to lower him to the ground. Handlers on the platform passed him awkwardly to those below,

133

and someone barked for the others to be careful as the vet's chair tipped and his forearms gripped its sluing, collapsible sides.

Should the lobbyist approach the man? Take it upon himself to "say it?" Strangely, he thought he might. What would he say then? Maybe, "You know, you're right. We were wrong. We let our egos mislead us. At least I did."

But why such a dramatic gesture? Maybe the vet deserved that much. It didn't matter how the gesture would be received, the lobbyist decided.

The lobbyist started walking down into the hollow before the Wall. His step quickened as he saw the vet being wheeled toward a waiting minivan.

The paraplegic's admirers began to clear out as the vet and his caretakers waited for the van's hydraulic lift to lower.

The lobbyist thought he might just reach him. He began to trot and then to run—his gouty limp easing.

Saying It

THERE IS ALWAYS SOMETHING IN MY LIFE I CANNOT NAME. It's the background to all the problems. Those who love me best provide strong hints to its proper name, opening my eyes to personal failings that are contact points with the mystery. My failings are pertinent, I find, but not in aggregate the whole. My life is shadowed by something even worse. Not problems, but the problem. Its existence at every point proves the key— for it's strange that as much as I try to "get on top of things," I find myself always in their midst. In the end, I've concluded, the perplexity must be me.

Even those who wouldn't want to admit as much have a great sense of how this operates in others. Those who have power in our lives often maneuver so that any criticism becomes difficult to voice. We cannot remind Aunt Millie of her disastrous first marriage or we will be cut out of her will. I don't want to tell Mom she's drinking too much because then she'd become angry and withdraw. The boss doesn't want to hear it, which is why, I suspect, he's asked me to report to my former peer, Dan. My teenager doesn't listen to me and, if I insist, she'll run away.

How many times do our relationships involve such bargains with the Devil? This is the great age of openness and honesty and yet I cannot imagine the reader not knowing exactly what I'm talking about. Names of people in the reader's own life come to mind, I'm sure.

From where does all this alienation among people come?

There aren't too many choices about how we answer this question. We can admit that our humanity consists of a fight against our own inhumanity, or we can claim exemption from the common failing by virtue of one idea or another about why we are right while others remain wrong.

Today friends are expected to support us by serving as an uncritical Greek chorus. Psychotherapy has proclaimed a universal dispensation from personal failure by teaching that we are all good at heart and do the best we can when not overwhelmed by environmental or genetic factors. So the thing for friends to do is listen sympathetically and approve or console. Away with judgment! Away with censure! We will know nothing of these. Once again, that valley of the shadow is strictly out of bounds.

What are people talking about in these conversations? What are friends being asked to support? Most often, I think, variations of what the Pharisees of Jesus' day understood as The Law. That is, when people talk to supportive friends, they give voice to their own standards: what they hope to achieve at work, in romantic relationships, or with their employers, coworkers, friends, relatives, and children. We speak of these things mostly as if we know what should be done in each instance, if only others would recognize the true nature of the situation. Or if we do not know what should be done, we don't want advice; we want listeners who will hear us out until we've arrived at the solutions for ourselves.

If we listen long enough to others, we can usually come up with their list of Personal Commandments. In my own life I used to live—and still do to a great degree—by these requirements:

- I must marry a woman beautiful enough to be the envy of my friends.
- I must make enough money to provide for my family in such a way that I will be seen as a good provider.
- I must publish a critically-acclaimed novel before I am thirty.
- I must publish a master work like James Joyce's *Ulysses* in the prime of my life.
- I must remain trim and active throughout my life and never have to retire.
- I must be a true champion of the dispossessed and never forget, despite my own wealth, their needs.
- My politics on every issue must be impeccable, which hindsight will clearly reveal as I become older.
- I must develop lifelong friends and struggle for common beliefs with them.
- I must never cease learning.
- I must understand the true nature of life and reality and be at peace before I die.

When I talk with my friends, I ask them to help me keep track of how I'm doing with this personal religion. Actually, most often, I'm asking them to verify that I'm doing just fine with it. And woe betide the friend who suggests that my aims are based on an underlying and entirely false conception of my true purposes in life and my abilities.

What would I say if someone were to infer, "You don't care anything about the dispossessed. Or if you do, it's only because such caring allows you to think better of yourself."

Or what would I say if my friend countered, "You'll never write a *Ulysses*. In fact, Louis L'Amour makes you look like a chump."

I so desperately want to be right. I so desperately want to be better than I really am. I want these things so much I succumb to the temptation of pretending they are true. I pretend to be something I'm not for goals and aims I don't even care about. The ones I do care about concern me and me alone and drive my pretensions.

I am comforted only in this: that Jesus says everyone does this and describes a radically simple solution to the problem. To this end he tells a parable directly for the benefit of those who would think better of themselves.

> "Two men went up to the Temple to pray, one a Pharisee and the other a tax collector. The Pharisee, standing by himself, was praying thus, 'God, I thank you that I am not like other people: thieves, rogues, adulterers, or even like this tax collector. I fast twice a week; I give a tenth of all my income.' But the tax collector, standing far off, would not even look up to heaven; but was beating his breast and saying, 'God, be merciful to me, a sinner.' I tell you, this man went down to his home justified rather than the other. For all who exalt themselves will be humbled, but all who humble themselves will be exalted."[1]

We are so familiar with the religious hypocrite that we take the Pharisee's words with too much doubting-salt, I'm afraid. Unlike most of us when we brag of keeping our Personal Commandments, the Pharisee probably has done exactly what he claims. The audience to whom Jesus told this parable wouldn't have considered the virtue the Pharisee claims for himself extraordinary; in fact, they would have seen his statement as simply factual. Just as we might see our own statements about our deeds and intentions as simply factual. But Jesus says the Pharisee is not justified before

God. Therefore he must be missing something—not in his actions, but in his attitude and viewpoint. In believing that he is right, does he inevitably miss those areas where he is wrong? The point of his prayers, as Jesus points out, should be to locate himself within his bewildering failures—to experience his "lostness."

On the other hand, the tax collector, a despised collaborator with an occupying government, is reconciled to God by his prayer. His income derives from his ability to cheat people of his own race for his own benefit and that of the Roman oppressor; this gives him the great advantage of being unmistakably in the wrong. He knows he's no good—evidently something, by Jesus' account, we are all required to recognize and ask forgiveness for.

I hope "The Vet and the Lobbyist" awakens our sense of how Jesus asked his audience to identify with someone they despised—to see themselves as the despised. The lobbyist presents the same imaginative difficulties, I suspect. The story also seeks to revive the dormant sense in us that whatever identifies us with the lobbyist, whatever area of our lives is fraught with bad motives, a sham constructed by the self's publicity machine, must legitimately respond to a call to "Say it!" That's Jesus' call: "Say it!" Because of God's image in which we are made, we know at a deep level that faults, to be forgiven, must be expressed, however reluctant we are to apply this understanding to ourselves.

Whether leftists or rightists, chic or square, abject failures or spectacular successes, we have to find whatever in our lives identifies us with the one calling, "God, be merciful to me, a sinner!" Then give voice to that same plea.

In the classic works of Christian spirituality, across the widest possible spectrum, the time of drawing close to God is preceded by the deepest possible experience of the person's distance from God. This time of recognition may occasion a distress that's like the grief of someone whose love for another person is not requited.

Truly sensitive souls often have an experience analogous

to the unrequited lover when they see the depths of God's love and their own distance from it. This is not the immediate searing of guilt that comes when we've committed a single egregious act—our panic at being caught stealing from our mother's purse or yelling at our spouse. No, it's not reactionary and brief but seasonal. Many of the great holy men and women of Christianity have, on their way to God, gone through a prolonged time of deep mourning at God's presumed loss. They feel an awareness at last of the one being they have always longed for, only to understand they have already, by their own actions, irrevocably cut themselves off from that person. They become so highly aware of their own failings that they find themselves detestable, agreeing with the type of judgment most of us reserve exclusively for others.

William James, whose *The Variety of Religious Experience* still provides ample material for reflection, quotes two people who passed through this experience on their way to spiritual conversion. One says, "[I] had been seeking, praying, reforming, laboring, reading, hearing, and meditating . . . [yet] I did not think I was one step nearer than at first, but as much condemned, as much exposed, and as miserable as before." Another puts it this way: "It was most unquestionably shown me, in one second of time, that I had never touched the Eternal: and that if I died then, I must inevitably be lost. . . . The Spirit of God showed it to me in ineffable love; there was no terror in it; I felt God's love so powerfully upon me that only a mighty sorrow crept over me that I had lost all through my own folly."[2]

In T. S. Eliot's poem "The Love Song of J. Alfred Prufrock," a bit of dialogue evokes the strangeness of how our own failings are always present to us and yet also beyond our control or even full imagining. In reply to a lover's anxious question, a woman turns her face away and says, "That is not what I meant at all. That is not it at all."

Don't we know that the same could be said to us, at almost every moment of our lives, with full justification? We sense that, despite our best intentions, the "good we would do, we do not," as St. Paul writes. Beyond even this, we all encounter in the revelations of other people (at least, if we are fortunate in their honesty), how we have utterly failed to anticipate what they often need most from us. From the man who says the wrong thing to his wife at the worst possible time to the woman who cannot see her husband's need of comfort to the friend who idly claims a prize—a team captaincy, a choir solo—that dashed the hopes of another. We constantly perpetrate crimes and misdemeanors whose very existence escapes us, except through our fitting dread of someone saying, "That is not what I meant at all. That is not it at all."

After I had sinned against God in a punishing, habitual way through drinking, I would certainly not have blamed God if God had said, "That is not what I meant at all. That is not it at all." Dispensing with my denial at last and recognizing I had by my own actions put my spiritual life to death, I was every bit as horrified at my distance from God as William James's penitents.

It doesn't even take the more spectacular varieties of sin to make a person aware of his or her distance from a holy God. In one of Peter's early encounters with Jesus, the Master suggests that Peter and James and those fishing with them row out once more. They object: "We have been fishing all night and caught nothing."

"Throw your nets to the other side," says Jesus.

The catch they bring in nearly swamps their boat. Peter falls on his knees before Jesus and cries, "Depart from me, Lord, for I am a sinful man."

What has Peter done wrong? Nothing in particular. Like the tax collector, he recognizes how distant his own nature must be from Jesus'. He calls out for mercy. He "says it."

The Lord tells him to get up on his feet. From now on, Peter will be fishing for men. This sinner will not only be justified but even taken into God's kingdom and made part of its creative action.

As a lover God does not spurn those who have betrayed him. God actually *insists* on making such people—and only such people — his company, his bride. Acknowledging the grounds on which we might be rejected becomes the means by which we are reconciled. We have to say it. That's what we must do: admit that Jesus has our number and ask for him to do for us what we cannot do for ourselves, reconcile us to God. "If we confess our sins, he who [Jesus] is faithful and just will forgive us our sins and will cleanse us from all unrighteousness."[3]

Instead of accusing us by saying, "That is not what I meant at all," Jesus reassures us that "anyone who humbles himself will be raised up."

We shouldn't be misled that this is easy. It has the broadest implications. Because the central drama of turning to God — especially, I think, in our time — consists not so much in being metaphysically sick at heart as it does in encountering our stubborn will to remain in control. Like Milton's Satan, we find ourselves preferring to rule in our own hells rather than serve in heaven. My favorite account of a contemporary person battling his own willfulness can be found in the spiritual autobiography, *The Golden String*, by Bede Griffiths. I love this account so much because Griffiths pursues his spiritual quest as a thoroughly modern person, one who is virtually unacquainted with guilt.

In the 1930s, Griffiths and two friends take a little house in England's Cotswolds at Eastington, determined to live as simply as possible. They believe in a religion of reawaking the imagination and what later generations would call "getting in tune with nature." When Griffiths isn't fetching water from the village or milking the cow, he reads. He progresses from the Romantic poets, through philosophy, to the Old and New Testaments of the Bible. Gradually, he becomes convinced that the glory he sees in nature is a reflection of God. The God he is coming to know has a personal will. The earth testifies not only to God's glory but also to his moral character.

Griffiths' experiment in living with his two friends lasts less than a year, but afterward, when his friends choose married lives on conventional family farms, Griffiths continues to seek being "alone with the alone." He thinks about becoming an Anglican priest, tries urban ministry, then returns to the Cotswolds for more solitude. He undertakes stringent periods of prayer and fasting. Completely to his own surprise, he finds himself saying over and over, "I must repent; I must repent." I always laugh when I get to this point in the book. Griffiths has a wonderful way of conveying the modern person's suspicions that any such impulse toward "repentance" must mean he is going out of his mind. Yet this impulse persists and Griffiths pursues it. He finally sees its reason:

> At Eastington I had been led through the asceticism, which our way of life forced on us, to break with the material world and to control my natural feelings and appetites. Then in the painful struggle in prayer during the night with the Cowley Fathers, I had been brought to renounce my own reason. Now I was made to renounce my own will. I had struggled against it and felt it as an invasion of my being by an alien power. There was indeed something terrifying in this power which had entered into my life and which would not be refused. It had revealed itself to me as love, but I knew now that it was a love which demanded everything. . . .[4]

Ultimately, "saying it" means not only confessing to individual actions that oppose God's will but through these regrets acknowledging that we are not our own. To be God's people we have to accept the idea that we are his children, renouncing control of our own lives for God's infinitely better way. We may feel, as Griffiths does, that this is courting madness. At this point in our conversation with Jesus we will surely be whispering or crying out in the dark.

SECTION IV
LIVING

CHAPTER ELEVEN

WHAT DOES IT MEAN
TO BE JESUS' FRIEND?

IF WE HAVE ACTED ON JESUS' DEMAND TO STAND BEFORE GOD and confess our failures—to identify our inability to keep from causing harm to ourselves and others—then what happens? Jesus says that the tax collector goes away "justified." What does this mean? How is it experienced, if it is? Do those who are justified know it?

In the Gospel accounts, Jesus claims the ability to forgive sins repeatedly. In fact many of the miracle accounts serve expressly as outward signs of an inward forgiveness. In one famous incident, the friends of a paralytic, unable to make their way through the crush of people into the home where Jesus is teaching, take their afflicted friend up to the home's roof. They make a hole in the roof through which they lower their friend into Jesus' presence.

Taking the extravagant gesture of lowering the man through the roof as a sign of faith, Jesus says, "Friend, your sins are forgiven."

Jesus' opponents, the Pharisees, are in attendance. The Pharisees wonder, "Who can forgive sins but God alone?"

Jesus sees their doubt and confusion and asks them, "Which is easier: to say, 'Your sins are forgiven,' or to say, 'Get up and walk'?" Then he heals the man, in order to make clear that "the Son of Man has authority on earth to forgive sins."[1]

The paralytic experiences his physical and spiritual healing in a flash. That seems as much the exception as the rule. Experience teaches us that any journey toward reconciliation, whether human or divine, may include a time of waiting, of quiet, of absence. We make our significant gesture. Something seems to have happened. But has it? We may wonder if our examination of conscience has been sufficient. Has our prayer been heard? Is there anything else to do?

We may even wonder whether this survey of our own darkness has turned out to be unnecessary, a useless indulgence in guilt; we might suspect that this is all going to be used against us or that we have used bad information against ourselves—to no purpose.

So am I truly reconciled now? I imagine my weapons industry lobbyist feeling more lost than ever after his embarrassed confession to the paralyzed veteran. What was that all about? Was it worth it? What now?

The Scriptures say that just before Jesus departed from his disciples for the last time, he told them to return to their common meeting place and wait. The Comforter, the Holy Ghost, was going to come to them. The Spirit would show them what to do and lead them into all truth.

They had no idea what he was talking about. They couldn't have—no more than we can know exactly how God may declare his forgiveness to us. In the disciples' case, Jesus had risen from the dead, and come back to them. Now he was choosing to leave again, but this time with the promise that God would be with them, in the person of the Holy Ghost. In fact the presence of this person in their lives would be better than Jesus' own presence. But how could this possibly be? What could he mean?

Most of those who become convinced of Jesus' teaching and the necessity of his death and resurrection enter into the mystery of these questions through waiting. Like Beckett's Vladimir and Estragon, the person has "kept his appointment" to the point of complying with the sole condition of the invitation, showing up in the filthy rags of "saying it"—confession. Now the question, "What does it mean to be reconciled?" becomes the person's intersection of time and space, where they are and who they are. How will God respond? How will God answer?

I remember this place in my own life, the strange stillness. What's starting? I wondered. Is it a new experience of abandonment or an unaccountable embrace? Another kind of death in this life or an unbelievable experience of living in the midst of such a deathly world? The strange quiet continued, accompanied by a certain lightness, an easing like the lobbyist's partial deliverance from gout.

I waited and watched, alert to what might follow. What is that? I might have asked. That sound? A conductor's baton tapping the music stand? An unseen river playing against the rocks beyond those trees? A stirring of wind in the treetops? I had the sense of my prayer going outward in the real hope that it would travel back to me somehow, as a mountain echo or the plink of a pebble finding the well's bottom.

Was my gesture at faith being rejoiced over by the unseen? Was someone calling my name? How long did I have to wait to find out? And how would I find out, if at all?

WE'RE HAVIN' A PARTY

THE FAMILY CONSIDERED THE OLD TYCOON'S BIRTHDAY CELE-bration a command performance. Every year Morty Zane's children and grandchildren and great grandchildren, along with the principal executives of the many companies he owned, took over a whole floor of The Fairmont Hotel atop Nob Hill in San Francisco. His many nieces and nephews came as well, and everyone who was married brought the whole family. People flew in from Cyprus, Belize, San Juan, Anchorage, Dubai, and almost every other point on the face of the globe, for the tycoon's wealth and influence had already obtained places for clan members among the world's movers and shakers. The Gettys, Van Leers, De Bartolos, Kuykendahls, Nordstroms, and many other families from San Francisco's elite also came. Everyone always declared the birthday bash a grand affair and were happy to pose for the *Chronicle*'s photographer.

In the past year the tycoon had taken a new wife. Married for fifty-five years to his aristocratic first wife, Laura Eve, the old man had abruptly ended five years as a widower by asking the woman who cut his hair, Cindy, to be his bride.

The haircutter was not the fresh, young, buxom thing his relatives imagined when they heard the horrifying news. She looked like an aging Las Vegas showgirl whose hard living showed. She kept her henna-and-frost hair piled on top of her head, penciled in her eyebrows, coated her false eyelashes with tarantula brown mascara, and wore heavy foundation makeup that quickly disappeared into large pores. She remained tall, thin, and long-limbed enough to carry herself with pride, though, and even the way the once-good lines of her face and figure swelled, puffed, and sagged had its own degenerate appeal. Her voice had been cured by Pall Malls and bourbon, and, when angry, she could blister the air. Her conversation ran to horse races and reminiscences about small-time hoods.

To justify what he had done, the tycoon would say only, "I liked the way she massaged my scalp."

This was too good an invitation for jokes for almost anyone to refuse; the tycoon became a laughing stock to his fashionable friends and a scandal to his relatives.

Cindy seemed to go out of her way not to help matters any. Unlike most gold diggers, she didn't aspire to become part of her husband's circle. She didn't accommodate herself to them either. She went on cutting hair. In her off-hours she took the old man bowling! She began dressing him in plaid shirts and work jackets and saw that he had a Scots tam on his head when he went out into the San Francisco fog and damp. They spent their evenings, it was rumored, watching "Wheel of Fortune" and playing canasta.

This year's invitation included the announcement that Cindy would be arranging their entertainment with many surprises in store. Morty wanted to use this party to reconcile his family to his new wife, to show them how great Cindy was.

No one found Cindy's new role encouraging, but most accepted the invitation anyway. They didn't want to alienate their meal ticket.

As the event neared, however, people began begging off.

The socialites withdrew first. Typical of the reasons advanced was this voice-mail from Everett Birsten: "Ginny and I would love to be there, Mort, as you know. We had planned on it. But CoMega's initial public stock offering is scheduled for earlier in the week, and I can't get away."[2]

The distant relatives slunk back next. Their excuses were closer to home—or at home. His nephew Bob called to say that Nancy and he and the kids had just moved into a new house. "Some of the finishing work is still being done, Uncle Morty. The tile the builder put into the kitchen should have gone into a house a block over, not ours, and they are correcting the problem now. We have to stay to make sure these idiots get it right this time."

Then his children and grandchildren and principal executives all discovered other family events. Morty Jr. said, "Emily's graduating from Stanford the weekend before, and then we're taking her and her boyfriend to Venice for a week. This is a once-in-a-lifetime thing, Dad. We'll see you next year."

Morty and Cindy had rooms reserved for one hundred and dinner and dancing planned for two hundred in The Fairmont ballroom.

"We're down to thirty-five guests," Cindy told Morty one afternoon. "We can't go through with our plans, can we?"

"Sure we can. There's even more reason to now."

"But Morty, what about the 'entertainment?' We can't really do it if they don't show up."

"We'll do it with those who do show up."

"That much for the thirty-five?"

"No, I want it spread around more than that. I want you to invite as many of your close friends as you'd like."

"But Morty if we . . . they'll really hate us then."

"I haven't asked much of you, Cindy, have I?"

"Not a swindler's marker, Honey."

"Do this then. For me."

So Cindy invited every showgirl-turned-beautician, alchy blackjack dealer, and racetrack exercise boy she had ever considered more than an acquaintance. Not a few invitations went to halfway houses, where their recipients immediately began requesting chaperoned furloughs.

That brought the list up to 150.

"I want street people!" Mort declared. "Go down to the Tenderloin. Get the kids who have run away and started hustling."

The birthday party was a formal affair, so each of the latter-day guests received a shower, haircut (from Cindy's girlfriends), make-over (whatever was needed), and a gown or tuxedo. They all dined sumptuously on a seven-course meal, while the wine flowed and members of the San Francisco Symphony played selections from Palestrina, Bach, Handel, and Vivaldi.

When the time for dessert arrived, Morty stood and asked for everyone's attention. "This is the moment I've been living all my life for," Morty said. "Gentlemen, if you would bring out the cake."

Four broad-shouldered men in white dinner jackets rolled in a cart on which sat the blue triple spires of Morty Zane's corporate headquarters, reproduced in an unbelievably light and flavorful rum cake. "I'm going to ask each of you," Morty said, "to wait until everyone has been served before partaking."

Quickly, large pieces of the cake were distributed to all two hundred in attendance by an army of stewards.

"This cake represents the business I've built over the years," Morty said. "It's me. My sweat and blood.

"And I'm giving it to you. Each one in attendance today at this party will go away entitled to the dividends on 1,000 shares of Zane Enterprises. At my death you'll control the principal of the shares and can sell them or keep them as you like. Cindy and I . . . Could you stand up, my bride?"

Cindy stood, towering over the stoop-shouldered tycoon. She bent to kiss his cheek, then wrapped both her arms loosely around his neck and clung there.

"Cindy and I wanted to end all the mystery about who was going to get what. We invited the rightful heirs, but most of them have chosen to look down on certain people. I'm glad at least some of the relatives came. Congratulations! You've made it to what you've long been promised. The rest of you are now my adopted sons and daughters—my heirs. Enjoy it! It's a gift I've given my life to bestow. And nothing, I assure you, has ever made me happier!"

Morty held up his plate and took a bite. "It's mighty good cake, too. L'Chayim!"

As the guests departed, shaking Morty's hand, a few of the old man's relatives in attendance asked about their relations. Did he have any plans to send along their shares?

"It's all gone. They missed it," Morty said.

"They did?"

To which the old man shrugged, cocked his head, and replied, "Their choice."

Living in the Here and Now
of Forever

IN OUR OWN TIME OF WAITING, WE MAY WONDER WHY WE have felt the need of being reconciled to God. Why has this become of paramount importance to us? Enough to risk making perhaps foolish metaphysical gestures, voicing our prayers to the silence.

Behind every essential question lies the desire to live: to live well, to live better, to keep living. How shall we do this? That's what our questions are all about.

We know we are going to die and yet we must constantly act as if this were not the case. In *The Denial of Death* Ernest Becker argues that keeping ourselves from being aware of our mortality is a necessary delusion; we cannot exercise ourselves to stave off death if we are overwhelmed by its final victory. We cannot enjoy the time that is given to us if that time is too heavily shadowed by its end.

Yet, unlike other creatures, we do not have the luxury of living unself-consciously. A deer hearing the crack of twigs close by fears harm; she does not shudder at the specter of non-existence. But Hamlet says,

> To sleep—perchance to dream: ay, there's the rub,
> For in that sleep of death what dreams may come
> When we have shuffled off this mortal coil,
> Must give us pause.[3]

What if in dying we experience horror? More exactly, the notion of death itself brings its own horror, not merely the fear of pain but a rebellious angst that all our triumphs and defeats, loves and losses, and what these have made us, our very selves, will no longer count. We are able to contemplate the prospect of our lives being extinguished and that seems horribly wrong, unjust. Within our most searching thoughts about mortality we find our immortal longings. We want to live forever. This desire actually provides the context in which we live, gives everything else meaning.

What if we could live forever? What if we are destined to? What if the supposition that we will not die were not, as Becker describes it, a "necessary psychosis" but a clue to our true natures as immortal creatures? Further, what if true immortality could begin in the context of mortality—the here and now? What if we as natural creatures could begin to live not merely in the context of immortal longings but on immortal terms— on a supernatural plane? To escape being our own perplexity, the problem or death we carry everywhere with us, and act in a way that's fully alive and brings life to others? How could such a life begin and be sustained? What food would it require?

When Jesus speaks of the life he means to extend through reconciling us to God, he talks about sharing a great banquet with us. He tells one of his greatest stories in the context of an actual dinner discussion.

One of the dinner guests, on hearing this, said to him, "Blessed is anyone who will eat bread in the kingdom of God!" Then Jesus said to him, "Someone gave a great dinner and invited many. At the time for the dinner he sent his slave to say to those who had been invited, 'Come; for everything is ready now.' But they all alike began to make excuses. The first said to him, 'I have bought a piece of land, and I must go out and see it; please accept my regrets.' Another said, 'I have bought five yoke of oxen, and I am going to try them out; please accept my regrets.' Another said, 'I have just been married, and therefore I cannot come.' So the slave returned and reported this to his master. Then the owner of the house became angry and said to his slave, 'Go out at once into the streets and lanes of the town and bring in the poor, the crippled, the blind, and the lame.' And the slave said, 'Sir, what you ordered has been done, and there is still room.' Then the master said to the slave, 'Go out into the roads and lanes, and compel people to come in, so that my house may be filled. For I tell you, none of those who were invited will taste my dinner.'"[4]

Jesus' story of the great banquet is provoked by someone speaking of "the meal in the kingdom of God." The speaker alludes to Judaism's "messianic banquet": the vision of life with God first envisioned by Isaiah. When the prophet foresaw the consummation of history, he saw a day of worldwide salvation, celebrated by luxurious feasting:

On this mountain the LORD of
hosts will make for all
peoples
a feast of rich food, a feast of
well-aged wines,
of rich food filled with marrow,
of well-aged wines strained
clear.
And he will destroy on this
mountain
the shroud that is cast over all
peoples,
the sheet that is spread over all
nations;
he will swallow up death
forever.
Then the Lord God will wipe
away the tears from all
faces,

and the disgrace of his people he
will take away from all the
earth,
for the LORD has spoken.
It will be said on that day,
Lo, this is our God; we have
waited for him, so that he
might save us.
This is the LORD for whom we
have waited;
let us be glad and rejoice in his
salvation.[5]

Yahweh soothes every hurt, brushes away every tear, and swallows up humankind's greatest enemy, death itself. He does so not only for Israel but for "every nation"—for all the world's peoples.

By alluding to the messianic banquet, the speaker who provokes Jesus' parable is voicing a pious sentiment. As the scholar Kenneth Bailey points out, Jesus might well have responded by saying something like, And we will be blessed too if we are found worthy to eat that meal in God's kingdom.[6]

Instead, Jesus claims the future banquet of humankind's salvation as his own, calling it "my banquet" in the wisdom statement that ends the parable. Through telling the parable, Jesus comments on who will be saved and why and what salvation will mean. He takes Isaiah's notion of a great banquet to which all nations will be invited and radically personalizes it, both in terms of the response required to the invitation and his own role in judging the fitness of that response. Jesus says that Isaiah's universal salvation—God's advent in bringing a worldwide justice—has now come to pass in his mission, for those who will receive it as such.

When I began thinking about the great banquet, my attention was drawn to an element that's not spoken of directly: the food. The banquet's menu figures into all the parable's meanings, both secular and spiritual.

155

When Middle Eastern hosts threw banquets, they always served a meat dish. The type of meat served depended on the number of guests coming. For a small party, one or two chickens, a duck for a larger one, then a lamb, and finally a calf. That's why Jesus' parable reflects a double invitation. The host cannot decide on the menu until he knows how many will be coming. After tallying his RSVPs, the host will slaughter a lamb or calf because this is meant to be a "great," or large, banquet.

The servant invites the man's natural peers — the other householders of the village, whose presence will bring the host honor, just as his invitation honors those he invites. All seems well as the man's intended guests accept willingly.

When his servant goes out to the invited guests to proclaim "all is ready," he's really saying, "Dinner is served." Like every host, the man giving the banquet must be anxious that his guests respond promptly. This is the moment he and his guests have been waiting for — a critical opportunity that must not be squandered.

But like the elder brother in the prodigal son parable, the first invited suddenly have second thoughts. Worse, while the elder brother's decision remains unknown, those who are invited to this banquet positively decline the invitation.

Then they come up with laughable excuses. When Jesus told this story, his audience no doubt smirked, then laughed aloud at the invitees' pathetic pleas. No Middle Easterner ever bought a parcel of land without inspecting every tree and bush and well and having these specified in the contract itself. No Middle Easterner ever bought one — let alone five — teams of oxen without handling their reins and testing their ability to pull together long before discussing price. The passionate newlywed can't even be bothered to ask forgiveness. He's busy, end of story. But even this rings untrue, as no host would schedule a banquet close to a wedding in a village. The man has been married at least for a time and his inability to spare a few hours from his honeymooning — particularly after having first agreed — means he's inventing an excuse as much as the others.[7]

What is the host to do with the food he has prepared — the fatted calf he has sacrificed? Like the father in the prodigal son parable, the host is offering the fruits of his *bios*, his living. In a way transparent to everyone, the invitees simply don't care about the host's banquet, which means that they cannot care greatly about the host himself. In fact, they are all too willing to insult him.

The story is essentially about what importance the guests attribute to the host — just as we take people's responses to our own invitations as indicating their regard for us. It's about those who accept the host and those who don't, those who embrace his life and its sacrificial giving as precious and those who turn away from it as unimportant. It's also about what the guests wish to make of their own lives. In Jesus' parable, the ungrateful invitees willingly make their lives about something other than their friendship with the host. Their excuses show how little they care.

That's not how they feel about their own lives, of course. It's all too clear that they care about their own affairs enough to insult the host — to let his living be sacrificed needlessly. Their self-interest holds sway.

The same applies in "We're Havin' a Party." Presumably, most of those who attend Morty Zane's birthday bash every year do so in order to live — to make a living, or to have the means of doing so. They want to inherit his money for the same reason. If they inherit a lot of his money, their lives, they may suppose, will be long and happy ones. Their inheritance dreams are like our own of winning the lottery or the Irish Derby.

But do they really care about Morty Zane? His scandalous second marriage tests their loyalty. What's more important: Morty himself, the money, or social prestige? We can make it up to the old guy next year, some may be reasoning, but for now let's steer clear of a socially damaging situation. Those who beg off care more about how others perceive them than how Morty does — even with a tremendous inheritance on the line.

157

(Oddly enough, they are probably being honest for the first time.)
The excuses of the invitees in the great banquet parable are such transparent lies that we have to wonder why they refuse to attend. The gospel writer Luke places the great banquet within the context of passages in which Jesus predicts his death and resurrection. When he's warned that Herod means to kill him, he says, "Go and tell that fox for me, 'Listen, I am casting out demons and performing cures today and tomorrow, and on the third day I finish my work. Yet today, tomorrow, and the next day I must be on my way, because it is impossible for a prophet to be killed outside of Jerusalem.'"[8]

As Jesus anticipates his journey to Jerusalem and his own death, he begins to articulate how people's decisions regarding his mission will determine their ability to be reconciled to God. When he arrives there, he says he will destroy the temple and raise it up again by the third day, meaning that he will willingly let himself be sacrificed and yet return from the dead, while at the same time replacing the focus of Jewish worship (the temple) with his own person. In John's gospel, he even says,

"Very truly, I tell you, unless you eat the flesh of the Son of Man and drink his blood, you have no life in you. Those who eat my flesh and drink my blood have eternal life, and I will raise them up on the last day; for my flesh is true food and my blood is true drink. Those who eat my flesh and drink my blood abide in me, and I in them. Just as the living Father sent me, and I live because of the Father, so whoever eats me will live because of me. This is the bread that came down from heaven, not like that which your ancestors ate, and they died. But the one who eats this bread will live forever."[9]

The host's story in the great banquet parable—even his menu—resonates with the hard words Jesus is speaking as he looks forward to his own sacrifice. Why do the invited guests turn away? The unanswered question was meant to provoke the audience's reflections on why people might turn away from Jesus himself. Did he embarrass them? Were they disappointed or scandalized by him? Did they find it impossible to believe that in this time, in this very place, the messiah had come? Was it too good to be true?

Early on in his ministry, Jesus finds it necessary to tell John the Baptist's disciples, "Happy are those who are not scandalized in me."[10] In this he's trying to comfort John as he sits in prison, waiting his own martyrdom. It's a way of saying, "Although it may be difficult for you to bear giving way to me and my ministry and paying such a heavy price, you will be blessed for doing so." He tells John to "keep the faith." John may not understand what Jesus is doing at the moment, the tactics he's employing, but John won't be disappointed in the eventual outcome. He wants to renew John's understanding that the messiah has indeed come.

In the same way each of us is blessed when we are not scandalized by Jesus; when we accept the banquet as his and our role as invited guests; when we are not ashamed to speak of him and believe in him as God's own Son, even to the point of suffering for it, from losing face in social settings to losing our lives when God's enemies become ruthless.

Because as invited guests we receive the "food of heaven," the presence of Jesus himself in our lives. This reality, this power, enables us, in the here and now, to begin living as the supernatural creatures we were destined to be. The reality of the kingdom of God, the life of heaven, begins in the midst of today when Jesus becomes present within us through the ministry of the Holy Spirit. Our aspirations for immortality — our desire to live — receives an earnest measure of its ultimate fulfillment: God changes us, God adopts us as sons and daughters. We may be the halt, the lame, and the blind. We may be outsiders to the community, hardly aware of the host, if at all — lost on our own endless byways. God takes in the crooks, the hustlers, the riff-raff and makes us his own. Like Morty Zane,

he extends a portion of his wealth to us in the here and now—
as much as we are capable of receiving. And he promises that
ultimately we will come into his inheritance entirely, where
we will know him as God knows us.

How does this happen? What's it like? What may lie on
the other side of our waiting?

Many people are still familiar with what Jonathan
Edwards called "surprising" works of conversion. The arche-
types of these experiences are established early in the history of Christianity. The doubter Thomas fingers Jesus' wounds
after the Resurrection, falls to his knees and proclaims, "My
Lord and my God." On the day of Pentecost, people from many
nations hear about Jesus in their own languages and rejoice
in ecstasy. The soon-to-be apostle Paul is blinded by a flash
of light in the midst of efforts to persecute the early church
and becomes the faith's foremost witness to the Gentiles.
These personal turn-arounds have been taking place in surprisingly similar ways ever since.

Jonathan Edwards's own accounts of such occasions during America's Great Awakening have always so fascinated me
that I can't help but relate one here. His account of Abigail
Hutchinson's conversion remains a classic.

This young woman goes through a time of heart-sickness,
of deep soul-searching.

> Her great terror, she said, was that she had sinned
> against God. Her distress grew more and more for
> three days, until (as she said) she saw nothing but
> blackness before her.

This time of crisis progresses until the turning point.

> When she went to bed on the Sabbath-day night, she
> took up a resolution that she would the next morning
> go to the minister, hoping to find some relief there. As
> she awaked on Monday morning, a little before day,

she wondered within herself at the easiness and calm-
ness she felt in her mind, which was of that kind
which she never felt before; as she thought of this,
such words as these were in her mind: "The words of
the Lord are pure words, health to the soul and marrow to the bones." . . . By these things her mind was
led into such contemplations and views of Christ, as
filled her exceeding full of joy.[11]

In my own life, I've had two distinct experiences that I
return to again and again as signposts of my pilgrimage. They
are far quieter than Mr. Edwards' account of Abigail
Hutchinson, but no less real, I think. (Neither applies exactly
to the initiation of my relationship with Jesus, which began
in my childhood.)

By the time I reached early manhood, I knew that either
I had to find God in a way that was real to me beyond anything that could be considered the product of my upbringing
or live my life as an agnostic. As many of the sons and daughters of the evangelical Christian world did in the 1970s, I jour-
neyed to a retreat center called L'Abri in the Swiss Alps, which
was run by the popular theologian and Christian apologist
Francis Schaeffer. In this idyllic setting, looking across a steep
green valley to a snaggle-tooth line of mountains called the Dents
du Midi, I called out to God, "Be real to me." I was not quite
twenty years old.

Until then I had tremendous trouble reading the New Testament. Every time I attempted to do so, my own intuitions
and doubts immediately started wrangling with what I had been
taught in my Christian household. For example, I wondered
why Jesus didn't confess more forthrightly to being the Messiah, even as the Bible teaching I had absorbed directed me to
the several passages where Jesus' status as the Christ is most
evident. I wondered about the different accounts of Jesus' life
in the Gospels and whether they were truly in harmony, as I
had been taught, or conflicted in important regards.

After praying "Be real to me," I started reading the Bible again and now it became to me "as meat and drink." I found tremendous pleasure and sustenance in it. Suddenly, I had an intuitive sense of why the "messianic secret" had to come into play—why Jesus could not have straight-out confessed to being the Christ. (He would have been killed straight off, as indeed he was killed when he made his status as the Son of God clear to his critics.) I also saw that my literary intuitions about the different purposes of the Gospel writers did not conflict with the truth of the gospel as a whole, but in fact, my literary intuitions could actually add to my appreciation of the gospel message.

This wholesale change in my reading of the Scriptures happened so quickly and so entirely that ever after I have thought of it as my most remarkable experience of the supernatural.

This revelation didn't keep me, however, from sinning gravely against the knowledge of what God had done for me, of course. I had been blessed in this fashion and then proceeded to become an alcoholic and a Valium addict.

My recovery from these addictions was also blessed with a sign that I remember as a perpetual marker. When I was about to come out of the treatment center, I had to decide whether to return to my teaching job in Wichita or resign and remain semi-attached to the treatment center and its outpatient recovery program. Valium addiction is a difficult thing to get over—much more difficult, physiologically, than alcohol. It robs the brain of its capacity to produce natural relaxants, as I was to find out through several months of teeth-grinding insomnia. My sister Mary was helping me return to health during this time, and I spent a long weekend at my brother-in-law Randy's and her house, praying as to what I should do.

People who know me personally know that in the best of times I'm a "high-wire act," someone given to worry and fear and care. (That's part of the reason Jesus' injunction, "Do not worry about your life," means so much to me.) Toward the end of my period of treatment, on furlough from the center during that weekend at my sister's house, I prayed, "I've really got to know what to do now, so show me." Obviously, my most authentic prayers are the most direct.

Jesus did show me. In the stress of withdrawal, with my muscles cramping, my back in such knots that I never wanted to come out of the shower, I had an unbelievable peace about returning to my job. My primary doctor at the center thought that would be okay, while most of the technical support staff doubted I would make it. But I had a genuine sense that I wasn't alone and that a divine power would carry me through.

I have prayed many times since for a similar peace and not found it. Often I have thought that the Lord has an outrageous understanding of what I can bear, if he does indeed abide by his promise not to test us beyond our capacities. Still, my sudden love of the Scriptures and my experience of peace in the midst of desolation are two moments in my life whose supernatural character I cannot doubt.

Whether God chooses to reveal himself to us in "surprising" or quiet ways, I'm convinced that God will reveal himself, in his own time and in his own way, to anyone who calls out to him directly and emphatically.

Beyond these spiritual markers of conversion, I've witnessed a confirming pattern in the lives of the Christians I've come to know, especially through my work as a journalist. Whatever the person's initial experience of a relationship with Jesus may be like, a dynamic reintegration of the person's character soon follows. Often one's most cherished goals in life look as if they must be abandoned only to be restored and fulfilled past the person's own imaginings in a new and better mode.

I'll cite one quick contemporary instance: the novelist Susan Howatch. A tremendous success as a commercial novelist, one who attracted praise as well for her craftsmanship, Howatch thought becoming a Christian, as she did in the mid-1980s, would mean the end of her writing career. She thought God would want her to give the craft up and devote herself to other pursuits. Instead, God called her into a much richer practice of that same craft—a greater fulfillment of the talent God had given her. Howatch has become a much better and more provocative novelist through her Church of England series, in which she examines questions of faith.

In Jesus' parable of "The Great Banquet," the profound desire for celebration in every person—for life to its fullest degree—is fulfilled at Jesus' banquet. Through the bread that comes down from heaven, one's hunger is not only satisfied, but one is given the power to be the person God intended. Whatever's wanting in a personality is left behind and the person is empowered to be him or herself in a way unexpected and yet prepared for by everything in life to date. As such, the work to which the follower of Jesus is called serves as an earnest of the person's citizenship in God's kingdom; it's both a sign of and a participation in that kingdom. The here and now begins to bear the glory of forever.

SO HOW DO WE GO ON WITH OUR LIVES?

LET'S SAY THAT GOD HAS TIPPED HIS HAND, DOFFED HIS CAP, and surprised and delighted us by letting us know that we've been seen, like Nathaniel, under our fig trees.[1] The signal of our reception into God's kingdom may have come through a friend's statement, a dream, a sudden experience of joy, or the church's means of speaking God's welcome through ceremony. After all, the church, although she may often appear like Morty Zane's Cindy—an aging showgirl with bad skin, bad taste, and bad associations—remains her bridegroom's chief help in throwing his reconciling party.

Like Peter we may now look around us and realize, yes, we've left our old lives behind to follow Jesus.

We may even begin to experience dynamic shifts in our personality—sometimes uncomfortable ones. C. S. Lewis, borrowing from George MacDonald, remarked that the new believer may anticipate the Christian life as a matter of having the foundations shorn up and the walls painted. Often the person finds himself in the midst of a wholesale reconstruction: a shack is being turned into a mansion and the process may entail plenty of destruction before the rebuilding begins.[2]

All of this may make us anxious about the rules of the game. What's this going to be like? How do we go on? Do we have to watch ourselves at every moment to make sure that we keep ourselves perfect? That's not likely to happen and probably we've already experienced its impossibility by lapsing into bad habits. The principal signal that we've begun to live in a new way may well be that we are suddenly conscious of how destructive our behavior can be in things both big and little.

The idea that we are now committed to a life of perfection or at least seeking something like it can be appalling. We may want to follow Jesus, but do we want to emulate the religious people who guard against living? If the point is life, then how do we go on with life in all its true passionate intensity, heartache, and fleeting happiness?

For some the most crucifying task may be to put up with sheer ordinariness, particularly if it means an ordinariness filled with unrelieved good behavior. Are we now committed to being do-gooders? People who abide by an ever-expanding list of instructions and injunctions and principles and rules?

On the other hand, some people who enter into this way often are all-too-ready to volunteer for obedience training. They want to show their commitment, to demonstrate their sincerity. Bring on the challenges. They are ready to rocket to super-holiness. As Jesus ascends into heaven, they are swimming eagerly through the air in pursuit.

How can anything so self-absorbed be right? But if these alternatives are wrong, we are left to ask: Is the Christian life then a matter of balance? Are we back to a little of this and a little of that and not too much of anything? Safe and sane once more! But now St. Safe and St. Sane. That doesn't seem right either.

How shall we follow you, Jesus? Is there a road map, a blueprint, a plan?

AUDITIONING

THE INTERNATIONAL MEGASTAR ANNOUNCED HIS NEXT PRO-
JECT would celebrate "the talents of ordinary people" because
he had always believed "music belongs to everyone who enjoys
it." He was staging a concert to be viewed via satellite from Lookout Mountain, Tennessee.

Why Lookout? He meant to demonstrate how much talent
and ability exists everywhere by selecting the stage crew, audio
technicians, camera operators, dancers, opening acts, and even his
own band members through open auditions. He didn't restrict the
auditions to Lookout Mountain residents—anyone could come to
try out from anywhere. He insisted, though, that auditioners be
amateurs or unknowns still working at their day jobs.

The event was to be staged as soon as it could be organized.
The star's advance people would arrive in the small town of
10,000 at the beginning of June to start the auditioning process,
gradually transferring authority to those selected.

Industry observers and critics reacted with surprise to the
announcement, as this megastar had built his worldwide following through performing in thousands of small venues. He
didn't do stadium shows. He was readily accessible, always
answering any question put to him, and yet the mystery of his
refusal to play the star surrounded him. He always appeared
without advance publicity, playing so many dates that his fans
accepted this impromptu scheduling. He didn't record himself,
but let anyone and everyone tape his shows. Bootleg copies (for
there were no other kind) of his performances filled the stores
and appeared regularly on MTV. His music, while thoroughly
contemporary, integrated musical idioms from classical to
country in such a disarming way that it inspired the deepest
longing. His concerts left people weeping and shattered and

often happier than they'd ever been in their lives.

Cynics speculated that the star selected Lookout Mountain because of its proximity to Nashville—there would be plenty of ringers to ensure a good show. In fact, so many aspiring musicians, actors, dancers, and entertainment industry "wannabes" found the offer irresistible that a migration began from every corner of the nation. This was a chance to rise from complete obscurity to global acclaim overnight. Who could resist?

The town of Lookout Mountain doubled in size the next day; by the time the star's advance team arrived, the surrounding area resembled a vast refugee camp, with RV encampments down every road and major tent cities on the west and south sides of town.

The city's goods and services became totally inadequate. Profiteers soon appeared, bringing semi-trailers of supplies into the area, charging quadrupled prices.

Many of the local grocers followed suit, but Bill Belzikian, who owned a small chain of stores, found the gouging contemptible and recruited townspeople and newcomers waiting on the audition lines into his operation to avert the crisis. The chain quickly geared up to meet the challenge and his reasonable prices vanquished the competition.

But this only led to water supply problems. Auditioners began opening up fireplugs and the city's municipal supply quickly drained to the point where a small fire could have burned the entire downtown section to a cinder. The chamber of commerce called on those outside the city limits to allow access to their private wells. The chamber issued guidelines on prices, but once again the profiteers took over before responsible citizens, such as Dale Thomas and Beatrice Gains, opened their own wells and distributed maps showing where to find the Wonderful Water Providers.

The auditioning process went slowly, with everyone being heard. The advance team gave few indications about the candidates that interested them. People became frustrated with so little information and many left, although others arrived daily to take their places.

The agonizing process of endless auditioning in the summer heat began to occasion mischief, with many thefts being reported, especially within the southside and westside tent cities where security was nonexistent. One of the auditioners, Mavis Palance, an out-of-work electrician and a tent city resident, organized a work crew to hook up floodlights to illuminate the tent city streets. She coordinated her team's efforts with the city's electrical utility, recruiting the necessary generators and fuel. Tent City Lights, as her crew came to be known, kept the floods in operation during the early evening hours when most of the crimes were being committed. Not only did these crimes decrease, but the "neighborhood" became more congenial as those with ill intentions moved on.

The whole auditioning phenomenon threatened to disappear as fast as it had come into existence when August 15 came and went. For some reason, the auditioners anticipated that the concert would be staged on or about the 15th.

The star's advance team pointed out that the star had said only "as soon as it could be organized." Many demanded that the star's team meet with the auditioning community in order to provide as much information as possible about their timetable and expectations for the event.

In the face of this demand, the star's team announced they had no timetable. They had been instructed only to hear auditions and make reports, instructions they had carried out from the beginning.

Many cried, "Fraud! Hoax!" Many went home. Others remained but fell into depression. A wave of flu swept the town and tent cities as well, with the first fall chills. In response, Dr. Julie Novotsky, Lookout Mountain's favorite pediatrician, organized Medics for Music. She set up a clinic to treat both somatic and psychological disorders, staffing it with townies and auditioners alike.

Garrett Brisbane, a bluegrass fiddler, thought another remedy might be music itself. Again, no one knew how, but the auditioning community came to expect that the concert would be held in the natural amphitheater located at Lookout Mountain's base. Garrett proposed that the audiences hold their own concert there.

A laconic man with the lean, angular body of a sentinel, Garrett's one or two words in the right quarters eventually induced a string of acts to line up for the free, auditioners' concert. A group of dancers, led by Vashti Boonswale, volunteered to perform as well. Garrett asked Mavis and her crew to run the lights and sound equipment. Bill Belzikian and his grocers, along with the Wonderful Water Providers, would transport enough food and drink out to the site for everyone to enjoy a feast. Dr. Novotsky's physicians—those who weren't playing—became security and emergency personnel.

As the pre-concert concert neared, Garrett was approached by more and more people in desperate financial situations. Could the event somehow become a benefit so that those with dwindling resources could stay to audition?

No admission charge, he said, but the hat would be passed.

The benefit idea actually encouraged all the participants. The auditioners came to feel a new solidarity with one another and took heart that however long the star might delay, they could persevere. They kept thinking, "Someday, someday soon, we're going global!"

The setting sun on the day of the benefit concert rained purple down on the big-shouldered mountain. The celestial stars came out in a big, blanketing sky as thousands walked into the amphitheater. Garrett and his Lemon Grass Crab Cakes led off the evening's entertainment.

As Garrett played a high-pitched two-string riff, he thought the group's bass player must be thumping out of tempo, then he looked up to see the chopping rotor-blade of a helicopter overhead.

It landed not two hundred yards away and out popped the star himself. His advance team rushed over and escorted him to the stage.

He immediately embraced Garrett. "Well done! Garrett!"

he said, when someone put a microphone in his hand. "And well done Bill and Dale and Beatrice and Mavis and Julie and Vashti and all those who have been working with them! You are the ones I want to do the show with!"

A great cheer went up and a swell of protest, too.

"But what about the auditioning process?" Garrett asked.

"You're on the stage, aren't you?"

"And the other acts?"

"Everyone who has volunteered. We'll play for ourselves tonight, and tomorrow we play for the world!"

"But what about us?" called some from the audience. "Don't we still get to audition? We came here to make music with you!"

"Is that why you came? I don't see any instruments in your hands. You're not helping with the lights, the sound, the spots, the emergency centers, or with crowd control. You haven't volunteered to dance. I have no idea why you came, but I'm sure it wasn't to make music."

"You mean it's over?"

"I'm afraid for you, it never started."

The star motioned for his guitar. "Okay, Garrett," he said, "let's play till dawn!"

Walking and Talking

JUST WHEN WE THINK WE HAVE THINGS FIGURED OUT, a strange double whammy seems to strike. "Auditioning" looks like one type of test and turns out to be another, without the rules ever being specified. What if we turn out to be those who did not understand what was being asked of us? Does this story bear any genuine relation to the teachings of Jesus? Again, this may strike us as unfair; if we have attempted to make our peace with God through believing in Jesus, then we may feel desperate that we will never understand the glossolalia or heavenly language of this calling.

"Auditioning" is based on a teaching from Jesus that's more a prophecy than a parable. But Jesus' rendering of the Last Judgment contains a working irony that adapts its meaning to the context of each life and clears away the false assumptions or worries we may bring to the way of Jesus. In the Last Judgment those who have failed to follow Jesus don't know what they've done wrong; those who have followed don't know what they've done right.

> "When the Son of man comes in his glory, and all the angels with him, then he will sit on the throne of his glory. All the nations will be gathered before him, and he will separate people one from another as a shepherd separates the sheep from the goats, and he will put the sheep at his right hand and the goats at the left. Then the king will say to those at his right hand, 'Come, you that are blessed by my Father, inherit the kingdom prepared for you from the foundation of the world; for I was hungry and you gave me food, I was thirsty and you gave me something to drink, I was a stranger and you welcomed me, I was naked and you gave me clothing, I was sick and you took care of me, I was in prison and you visited me.' Then the righteous will answer him, 'Lord, when was it that we saw you hungry and gave you food, or thirsty and gave you something to drink? And when was it that we saw you a stranger and welcomed you, or naked and gave you clothing? And when was it that we saw you sick or in prison and visited you?' And the king will answer them, 'Truly I tell you, just as you did it to one of the least of these who are members of my family, you did it to me.' Then he will say to those at his left hand, 'You that are accursed, depart from me into the eternal fire prepared for the devil and his angels; for I was hungry and you gave me

no food, I was thirsty and you gave me nothing to drink,
I was a stranger and you did not welcome me, naked and
you did not give me clothing, sick and in prison and you
did not visit me.' Then they also will answer, 'Lord, when
was it that we saw you hungry or thirsty or a stranger or
naked or sick or in prison, and did not take care of you?'
Then he will answer them, 'Truly I tell you, just as you did
not do it to one of the least of these, you did not do it to
me.' And these will go away into eternal punishment, but
the righteous into eternal life."[3]

The misunderstandings of both the blessed and the damned
in this passage reveal more about them than encyclopedic
accountings of their lives possibly could, for these misunderstandings reveal the essential motions of their hearts. The
blessed don't know they have been serving Jesus in the per-
sons of the "least of these." The damned believe they would
have served Jesus if they had only been given the opportunity.
They presume their hearts were in the right place, whereas the
blessed presume . . . what? Nothing about themselves. They have
been too busy acting as Jesus would have acted in their places.
Like the old and now revived saying, their one question has
been, What would Jesus do?

Life appears to be a test that's about succeeding or failing.
We can bring any understanding of morality to this context
without essentially changing the equation. We can be existen-
tialists and decide that life's about creating our own sense of meaning and then failing or succeeding in choosing faithfully what
we have previously decided to choose. We can be amoralists and
think life is about doing anything we please, as long as we can
get away with it, only to find ourselves not always serving our
own desires—even amoralists can be immoral, in this sense.
Or we can be religious and think that life's about obeying a list
of ethical standards, keeping the capital "L" law or our own lower-
case versions. Still we will succeed or fail by degree.

Jesus totally removes life—all of life—from the context of

success and failure. We don't have to obey a list of instructions, injunctions, principles, and rules. We don't have to watch ourselves every moment in the search for perfection. We also do not have to pretend that our emotional lives are something other than what they are, taking ourselves out of the common joys and heartaches of life for the sake of a transcendent boosterism, pretending that because God is in our lives nothing can move or trouble us. We do not have to fear ordinariness, either. Something's definitely afoot that will take us well out of ordinariness, at least to the extent allowed by earthly existence.

Life appears to have only two options: success or failure. These create our constant sense of dilemma. Which shall it be?

Jesus says neither. The blessed don't even know when they've done the right thing. How can this be?

Because the way of following Jesus is about following, just that and nothing more. Through the Holy Spirit, the Comforter, Jesus is as present—more present, by Jesus' own accounting—with today's believer than he was in the disciples' lives. So the way of following Jesus really is about doing what we've been doing here, in these chapters, these conversations: walking around with Jesus and asking him questions and then acting as his friend. It's about knowing someone. It's about loving someone who loves us. It's about taking up residence in God's world, believing that we live where God reigns, and because of this acting in a way that makes little sense to those who believe the world is a cosmic accident. It's about attending to all the ways the invisible things of God work to transform the visible. God's power becomes a given. God's love also. God's justice becomes the order that works to right the broken world's disorder.

Jesus ceases to be a historical figure with a baffling outlook and becomes the unseen guest, the silent admonisher, the one to whom we go to be held, embraced, and encouraged.

We begin to experience heaven on earth and enter into God's means of transforming the world; we allow ourselves to be incorporated into God's plans, into his reality.

We cannot know how this is going to happen and the not

knowing is crucial. Because if we *could* know, we'd draw up a list of rules and then make these the occasion of worshiping ourselves—as we saw in the parable of the Pharisee and the tax collector. Only the infinitely subtle nuance of relationship—of personal direction through the Scriptures, the church, and the testimony of the Holy Spirit within us—can steer us clear of our own egotism. Only by completely forgetting about ourselves and thinking only of Jesus can we enter into Jesus' present action within the world.

How shall we go on with life? Jesus tells us to follow him, to listen to him, to act as he would, and in all these ways and others, to love him. One way of looking at it is that the Christian life is all a conversation. I'd like to think this book reflects and even incorporates in its methods the manner of the Christian life—the way it's carried on. Christian spirituality is all about talking to God, meditating on the words of Scripture in order to hear God's voice, studying what we can know about the background and context of the Scriptures and how people have understood them in the past, and then taking all of this information again directly to God in more conversation. It's about learning how our questions of God become God's questions of ourselves. It's about examining how we are already in the midst of answering those questions through our beliefs and actions and then changing these if God shows us better answers. It's about never being content in this conversation until that ultimate day of felicity when we know God as he knows us—when our apprehension of God becomes immediate and total.

If we continue our conversations with Jesus in this way, we will find ourselves keeping God's commandments. We will find ourselves ministering to him in unknown guises. We will begin to see the face of Jesus in everyone because everyone in his or her humanity has the potential of joining Jesus in his divine life, and everyone needs to be assured of this through concrete demonstrations of love.

The road map, the blueprint, the plan will not only emerge

but also triumph, because it will be God's and not our own. Indeed, as we listen to and respond to our individual callings, we will find ourselves caught up into a vast community of believers who enjoy the most implausible and yet flawless coordination. I tried to indicate something of this through the way the concert comes together as if by chance in "Auditioning," while all along this "chance" has been constitutive of the star's plan. That's a way of saying only God can understand and plan for the macrocosm of history and time without discounting each individual's concerns. Only God can reconcile the needs of the person and those of the community. Indeed, God's love gathers itself and multiplies through his universal and timeless community.

Undoubtedly, the most compelling example of how God coordinates individual responses to his calling into a mighty chorus of witnesses exists in the Scriptures themselves. Here we have a "concert" that came about through individual responses to ever-shifting political and cultural conditions across thousands of years that yet tells a unified story of God inviting humankind back into relationship. In the Scriptures, the minimalist narratives of the Pentateuch join with the historical chronicles, the Psalms of David, the sometimes curdled views of the wise but surfeited Solomon, the apocalyptic visions of Daniel, the laments of Jeremiah, and the deeply resonant promises of Isaiah. Here the dramatic spareness of Mark, the elaboration of Matthew, the diagnostics of Luke, and the transcendent theology of John combine with the knotty reasoning of Paul, the pastoral considerations of Peter, and the consummate apocalyptic of John. All are bound together by the theme of God's offer of reconciliation. The skeptic may insist that all of these individual voices may be analyzed into profound disagreement and contradiction, but through the millennia those with "ears to hear" have received all of these voices as united with God's own.

Just so, our often scattered lives can be united with God's through his presence with us in Jesus Christ—the perfect reconciliation of God and humankind.

OPENINGS
WITHOUT END

"I FEEL SO DEAD INSIDE," I ONCE CONFESSED TO MY OWN astonishment and horror. Would I now exclaim, "I'm alive," with all the surprise and delight of the prodigal? Has this conversation, this encounter, with Jesus worked? Do I have not only an imaginative grasp of how Jesus seeks to establish heaven on earth but one that brings with it a transforming belief? And would I claim that God truly changes the world, reconciling people and cultures to himself through this individual yet universal process?

Sometimes I give talks about what it was like to be a professional Christian alcoholic, to walk among the living dead. Usually the groups I speak to are composed of well-turned-out retreat-goers, in pleated shorts with braided belts, the softest cotton blouses or shirts, and display-worthy cross-trainers: all clothed, in their right minds, happy, successful, prosperous, established. I'm never far into my confession when the well-scrubbed surface comes off and my own anxieties, depressions, wounds, pain, and sense of death touch the group's seared second skin. They know well what I'm talking about and often they're glad for a chance to acknowledge as much. I'm always tremendously moved by the painful accounts they give of their own lives.

This experience of shared pain takes place in the most sedate of settings. I've witnessed less decorous versions as well, from inner cities to Third World nations. Death, whether in disguise or through the blatant appearances of violence, malnutrition, and disease, stalks the world's life and brutalizes its joy.

We all know this, however much our means of access may differ.

So there's a great deal at stake here—in fact, everything that we cherish about life. Can we really step into the fullness of life, an eternal life, in the midst of a world stalked by death? Is this a pipe dream or the world's only true hope?

Recently I spoke with someone who had known me in the bad old days and we were now becoming friends again. He said, "When I knew you before, I thought you were the kind of person who might destroy himself. But you've grown out of that."

Not exactly, I thought. I did destroy myself. I can hardly hold myself up as an example of anything, except the inevitable destruction that comes with self-worship. The parts of Jesus' teachings I have verified through personal experience beyond any doubt comprise his understanding of the human person's alienation. We don't know what's in our own best interests. We make ourselves and everyone around us miserable when we act as if we do or could. The best and the brightest among us must be rescued from self-nomination to that egotistical category, or else, like Shakespeare's Gloucester, we will end by saying, "I stumbled when I saw"—I was the most blind when I thought I could see.

I also know and must confess that I have been restored to life in a significant way. There are even moments—for example, when a friend spoke of his own conversion after reading Isaiah 53, the passage that describes a man of sorrows, one acquainted with grief, who is bruised for our evils, and whose stripes heal us—when unexpected, joyful tears declare to me the beginnings of that transforming belief for which I have longed. It seems that I am growing into some measure of loving God.

And I know that just as Augustine and many other believers have achieved goals—in Augustine's case being a chief advisor to the emperor—that they burned out pursuing prior to their conversions, so I'm now able to use whatever talents I possess with a new freedom. I know that freedom comes in obedience and only in obedience. We cannot listen to our inner voices, our bliss, nor even set up the common implications of our inherent skills and talents as destiny. We have to be directed by another. Without a greater power to direct us, our lives can only be self-extinguishing: tapers of more or less brilliance feeding on themselves.

Jesus says, If you are determined to live your life in your own way, you won't have any life. But if you will live your life serving me, you will find life.

That's what we all want. I've found it a chance worth taking.

NOTES

Chapter 1—Opening

1. Vaclav Maly, Laszlo Tokes and Jerzy Popieluszko, all members of the clergy, were key leaders of the revolution in Eastern Europe in 1989.

2. I realize that biblical scholars often view the various forms of the parables as the use the individual evangelist is making of what are perhaps original sayings of Jesus—uses that are construed as being directed toward the early church. Jesus' commentaries are even more widely regarded, whether they are seen as simply situated next to the parable by the evangelist or in fact invented by the gospel writer, as showing the evangelist's purposes rather that Jesus' own. What I'm addressing here is the underlying pattern of question, story, and commentary, which has deep roots in the tradition of Jewish rhetoric within which Jesus must have taught. (See Joseph Heineman, "The Proem in The Aggadic Midrashim: A Form-Critical Study," SH 22 (1971), pp. 100-122, and Richard Stern, Parables in Midrash (Cambridge, Mass.: Harvard University Press, 1991). I do take the pattern in the gospel of dialogic teaching as being a true reflection of Jesus ministry, which I believe everything we know about Jewish rhetoric and the traditions of rabbinical teaching give us ample reason to assume.

Chapter 2—Is There a Loving God?

1. Carl Sagan, Cosmos (New York: Random House, 1979), p. 282.
2. Lyrics from "One of Us" by Eric Bazilian. Used by permission of Warner Bros. Records.
3. Luke 11:5-9.
4. Luke 11:13.

Chapter 3—What About Tragedy?

1. Luke 13:34.
2. Mark 4:3-9.

Chapter 4—Why Doesn't God Show Himself More Clearly?

1. Samuel Beckett, Waiting For Godot (New York: Grove Press, 1854), p. 51B.
2. 2 Samuel 5:2.
3. Psalm 23:1.
4. Luke 15:1-7.
5. Luke 15:8-10.
6. John 10:7,10-11.
7. John 14:6.

Chapter 5—*Who Are We?*
1. John Dominic Crossan, *The Dark Interval* (Sonoma, Calif: Polebridge Press, 1988), p. 39.
2. Perhaps this is why Jesus could use the imagery of being born again—to be born into God's reality and find a new self—so powerfully. Imagine how potent that would be for someone whose reality was almost totally proscribed by his or her birth.
3. This story is recorded in Mark 10:17-27.
4. Mark 10:21.
5. Mark 10:24-25.
6. "The Camel and the Eye of the Needle" strikes us more as a riddle than what we commonly think of as a parable. The original term *mashal,* which we translate "parable," encompassed almost any type of comparison, however short or extended. We are inclined to think of Jesus' parables only in terms of short fictions.
7. Matthew 19:29.
8. Luke 9:24-25.

Chapter 6—*How Can We Be Truly Free?*
1. As quoted in William H. Johnston, *Our Response to the Lord: Faith Sharing Options II* (New Jersey: Paulist Press, 1996), p. 26.
2. Luke 12:13-22.

Chapter 7—*Is God Fair?*
1. Matthew 17:24-27.
2. See Matthew chapter 5.
3. Matthew 6:21.
4. Matthew 20:1-16.
5. See Isaiah's "Song of the Vineyard," Isaiah 5:1-7.
6. Walker Percy, *Lost In The Cosmos* (New York: Farrar, Strauss, & Giroux, 1983), pp. 57-69.

Chapter 8—*How Good Do We Have to Be?*
1. Luke 10:25-28, NJB.
2. Sirach 12:1-6. As translated by Kenneth E. Bailey, *Through Peasant Eyes*, in the combined edition *Poet & Peasant* and *Through Peasant Eyes* (Grand Rapids, Mich.: Wm. B. Eerdmans Publishing Company, 1983), pp. 43-44.
3. Luke 10:29-36.
4. Kenneth E. Bailey, *Through Peasant Eyes* in the combined edition *Poet & Peasant* and *Through Peasant Eyes* (Grand Rapids, Mich.: Wm. B. Eerdmans, 1983), p. 52.
5. Matthew 5:17.
6. John 4:7-30: A Samaritan woman came to draw water, and Jesus said to her, "Give me a drink. (His disciples had gone to the city to buy food.) The Samaritan woman said to him, "How is it that you, a Jew, ask a drink of me, a woman of Samaria?" (Jews do not share things in common with Samaritans.) Jesus answered her, "If you knew the gift of God, and who it is that is saying to you, 'Give me a drink,' you would have asked him, and he would have given you living water." The woman said to him, "Sir, you have no bucket, and the well is deep. Where do you get that living water? Are you greater than our ancestor Jacob, who gave us the well, and with his sons and his flocks drank from it?" Jesus said to her, "Everyone who drinks of this water will be thirsty again, but those who drink of the water that I will give them will never be thirsty. The water that I will give will become in them a spring of water gushing up to eternal life." The woman said to him, "Sir, give me this water, so that

I may never be thirsty or have to keep coming here to draw water." Jesus said to her, "Go, call your husband and come back." The woman answered him, "I have no husband.' Jesus said to her, "You are right in saying, 'I have no husband"; for you have had five husbands, and the one you have now is not your husband. What you have said is true!" The woman said to him, "Sir, I see that you are a prophet. Our ancestors worshiped on this mountain, but you say that the place where people must worship is in Jerusalem." Jesus said to her, "Woman, believe me, the hour is coming when you will worship the Father neither on this mountain nor in Jerusalem. You worship what you do not know; we worship what we know, for salvation is from the Jews. But the hour is coming, and is now here, when the true worshipers will worship the Father in spirit and truth, for the Father seeks such as these to worship him. God is spirit, and those who worship him must worship in spirit and truth." The woman said to him, "I know that Messiah is coming" (who is called Christ). "When he comes, he will proclaim all things to us." Jesus said to her, "I am he, the one who is speaking to you." Just then his disciples came. They were astonished that he was speaking with a woman, but no one said, "What do you want?" or, "Why are you speaking with her?" Then the woman left her water jar and went back to the city. She said to the people, "Come and see a man who told me everything I have ever done! He cannot be the Messiah, can he?" They left the city and were on their way to him.
7. INFOPEDIA, © 1996 by SoftKey Multimedia, Inc., a subsidary of SoftKey International, Inc. The Merriam-Webster Dictionary of Quotations, © 1990 Merriam-Webster, Inc.
8. Galatians 3:24-29, MSG.

Chapter 9—*Is Grace Truly Amazing?*
1. 2 Peter 2: 8, KJV.
2. Luke 15:11-32.
3. See Luke 17:25 and following.

Chapter 10—*How Should We Respond to Jesus?*
1. Luke 18:10-14.
2. As quoted in William James, *The Varieties of Religious Experience* (Triumph Books: New York, 1991), pp. 177, 180.
3. 1 John 1:9, KJV.
4. Bede Griffiths, *The Golden String* (Springfield, Ill.: Templegate Publishers, 1980), p. 117.

Chapter 11—*What Does It Mean to Be Jesus' Friend?*
1. Luke 5:17-26: One day, while he was teaching, Pharisees and teachers of the law were sitting near by (they had come from every village of Galilee and Judea and from Jerusalem); and the power of the Lord was with him to heal. Just then some men came, carrying a paralyzed man on a bed. They were trying to bring him in and lay him before Jesus; but finding no way to bring him in because of the crowd, they went up on the roof and let him down with his bed through the tiles into the middle of the crowd in front of Jesus. When he saw their faith, he said, "Friend, your sins are forgiven you." Then the scribes and the Pharisees began to question, "Who is this who is speaking blasphemies? Who can forgive sins but God alone?" When Jesus perceived their questionings, he answered them, "Why do you raise such questions in your hearts? Which is easier, to say, 'Your sins are forgiven you,' or to say, 'Stand up and walk'? But so that you may know that the Son of Man has authority on earth to forgive sins"—he said to the one who was paralyzed—"I say to you, stand up and take your bed and go to your home." Immediately he stood up

before them, took what he had been lying on, and went to his home, glorifying God. Amazement seized all of them, and they glorified God and were filled with awe, saying, "We have seen strange things today."
2. The use of "CoMega" here is entirely fictional. No association with any real-world company is meant or implied.
3. Shakepeare, *Hamlet*, III.1. 65-68.
4. Luke 14:15-24.
5. Isaiah 25:6-9.
6. Kenneth E. Bailey, *Through Peasant Eyes* in the combined edition with *Poet & Peasant* and *Through Peasant Eyes* (Grand Rapids, Mich.: Wm. B. Eerdmans, 1983), p. 92.
7. I wonder whether the excuses thinning as they go along indicates possible peer pressure not to go. The first take the best excuses, the next, finding out the first won't be attending, make up weaker ones—the reverse of waiting to find out who's going before accepting an invitation.
8. Luke 13:32-33.
9. John 6:53-58.
10. Matthew 11:4, my paraphrase.
11. Jonathan Edwards, *A Faithful Narrative* in *The Works of Jonathan Edwards*, vol. 4, edited by C. C. Goen (New Haven, Conn.: Yale University Press, 1972), pp. 192, 193-194, 195.

Chapter 12—*So How Do We Go on with Our Lives?*
1. John 1:43-51: The day following Jesus would go forth into Galilee, and findeth Philip, and saith unto him, Follow me. Now Philip was of Bethsaida, the city of Andrew and Peter. Philip findeth Nathanael, and saith unto him, We have found him, of whom Moses in the law, and the prophets, did write, Jesus of Nazareth, the son of Joseph. And Nathanael said unto him, Can there any good thing come out of Nazareth? Philip saith unto him, Come and see. Jesus saw Nathanael coming to him, and saith of him, Behold an Israelite indeed, in whom is no guile! Nathanael saith unto him, Whence knowest thou me? Jesus answered and said unto him, Before that Philip called thee, when thou wast under the fig tree, I saw thee. Nathanael answered and saith unto him, Rabbi, thou art the Son of God; thou art the King of Israel. Jesus answered and said unto him, Because I said unto thee, I saw thee under the fig tree, believest thou? thou shalt see greater things than these. And he saith unto him, Verily, verily, I say unto you, Hereafter ye shall see heaven open, and the angels of God ascending and descending upon the Son of man. (KJV)
2. C. S. Lewis, *Mere Christianity* (New York: Simon & Schuster, 1996), p. 176.
3. Matthew 25:31-46.

AUTHOR

HAROLD FICKETT is the author of several nationally-acclaimed books, including *The Holy Fool* and *Flannery O'Conner: Images of Grace*. He compiled, edited, and introduced the recent *Things In Heaven & Earth: Exploring The Supernatural*. He co-founded *Image: A Journal of the Arts & Religion*. Currently, he writes full time and speaks, and can be reached via e-mail at HFickett@worldnet.att.net.

MORE NEW WAYS TO DISCOVER JESUS.

Stories of Jesus

Jesus didn't tell stories to entertain, but to reveal who
God is and draw us closer to him. Based on *The Message*,
a best-selling contemporary rendering of the Bible,
Stories of Jesus invites you to think and live
in ways that can change the story of your life.

Stories of Jesus
(Eugene H. Peterson) $12

Sayings of Jesus

Topically arranged from the text of *The Message*,
Sayings of Jesus presents the words of Jesus on a variety
of subjects, giving readers a clear understanding of what
Jesus said and clear direction for their actions.

Sayings of Jesus
(Eugene H. Peterson) $12

Get your copies today at your local bookstore,
through our website, or by calling (800) 366-7788.
Ask for offer **#2385** or a FREE catalog of NavPress resources.

NAVPRESS
BRINGING TRUTH TO LIFE
www.navpress.com

Prices subject to change.